MW00332933

LEADER'S GUIDE

Dr. Mary Jo Osterman is a Christian educator who serves as a freelance writer and editor. A lifelong United Methodist currently living in Colorado, Dr. Osterman has written United Methodist curriculum materials and has led numerous workshops and leadership training events on a variety of issues. Dr. Osterman is the writer of volume 5 of *Journey Through the Bible: 1 Kings—Esther.*

JOURNEY THROUGH THE BIBLE: MARK. LEADER'S GUIDE. An official resource for The United Methodist Church prepared by the General Board of Discipleship through the division of Church School Publications and published by Cokesbury, a division of The United Methodist Publishing House; 201 Eighth Avenue, South; P.O. Box 801; Nashville, TN 37202. Printed in the United States of America.

Scripture quotations in this publication, unless otherwise indicated, are from the New Revised Standard Version of the Bible, copyright ©1989 by the Division of Christian Education of the National Council of the Churches of Christ in the United States of America, and are used by permission. All rights reserved.

For permission to reproduce any material in this publication, call 615-749-6421, or write to Cokesbury, Syndication—Permissions Office, P.O. Box 801, Nashville, TN 37202.

To order copies of this publication, call toll free 1-800-672-1789. Call Monday—Friday 7:30—5:00 Central Time or 8:30—4:30 Pacific Time. Use your Cokesbury account, American Express, Visa, Discover, or MasterCard.

© Copyright 1994. All rights reserved.

01 02 03 – 10 9 8 7 6 5 4 3

EDITORIAL TEAM

Debra G. Ball-Kilbourne
Editor

Linda H. Leach
Assistant Editor

Linda O. Spicer
Adult Department Assistant

DESIGN TEAM

Susan J. Scruggs
Design Supervisor
Cover Design

Ed Wynne
Layout Designer

ADMINISTRATIVE STAFF

Neil M. Alexander
Vice-President, Publishing

Duane A. Ewers
Editor of Church School Publications

Gary L. Ball-Kilbourne
Executive Editor of Adult Publications

 Since 1789

Cokesbury

THIS PUBLICATION IS PRINTED ON RECYCLED PAPER

CONTENTS

Volume 10: Mark   **by Mary Jo Osterman**

INTRODUCTION TO THE SERIES

The leader's guides provided for use with JOURNEY THROUGH THE BIBLE make the following assumptions:
- adults learn in different ways:
  —by reading
  —by listening to speakers
  —by working on projects
  —by drama and roleplay
  —by using their imaginations
  —by expressing themselves creatively
  —by teaching others
- the mix of persons in your group is different from that found in any other group.
- the length of the actual time you have for teaching in a session may vary from thirty minutes to ninety minutes.
- the physical place where your class meets is not exactly like the place where any other group or class meets.
- your teaching skills, experiences, and preferences are unlike anyone else's.

We encourage you to discover and develop the ways you can best use the information and learning ideas in this leader's guide with your particular class. To get started, we suggest you try following these steps:

1. Think and pray about your individual class members. Who are they? What are they like? Why are they involved in this particular Bible study class at this particular time in their lives? What seem to be their needs? How do you think they learn best?
2. Think and pray about your class members as a group. A group takes on a character that can be different from the particular characters of the individuals who make up that group. How do your class members interact? What do they enjoy doing together? What would help them become stronger as a group?
3. Keep in mind that you are teaching this class for the sake of the class members, in order to help them increase in their faithfulness as disciples of Jesus Christ. Teachers sometimes fall prey to the danger of teaching in ways that are easiest for themselves. The best teachers accept the discomfort of taking risks and stretching their teaching skills in order to focus on what will really help the class members learn and grow in their faith.
4. Read the chapter in the study book. Read the assigned Bible passages. Read the background Bible passages, if any. Work through the Dimension 1 questions in the study book. Make a list of any items you do not understand and need to research further using such tools as Bible dictionaries, concordances, Bible atlases, and commentaries. In

other words, do your homework. Be prepared with your own knowledge about the Bible passages being studied by your class.
5. Read the chapter's material in the leader's guide. You might want to begin with the "Additional Bible Helps," found at the *end* of each chapter in the leader's guide. Then look at each learning idea in the "Learning Menu."
6. Spend some time with the "Learning Menu." Notice that the "Learning Menu" is organized around Dimensions 1, 2, and 3 in the study book. Recognizing that different adults and adult classes will learn best using different teaching/learning methods, in each of the three dimensions you will find
   —at least one learning idea that is primarily discussion-based;
   —at least one learning idea that begins with a method other than discussion, but which may lead into discussion.

   Make notes about which learning ideas will work best given the unique makeup and setting of your class.
7. Decide on a lesson plan: Which learning ideas will you lead the class members through when? What materials will you need? What other preparations do you need to make? How long do you plan to spend on a particular learning idea?
8. Many experienced teachers have found that they do better if they plan more than they actually use during a class session. They also know that their class members may become frustrated if they try to do too much during a class session. In other words
   —plan more than you can actually use. That way, you have back-up learning ideas in case something does not work well or something takes much less time than you thought.
   —don't try to do everything listed in the "Learning Menu." We have intentionally offered you much more than you can use in one class session.
   —be flexible while you teach. A good lesson plan is only a guide for your use as you teach people. Keep the focus on your class members, not your lesson plan.
9. After you teach, evaluate the class session. What worked well? What did not? What did you learn from your experience of teaching that will help you plan for the next class session?

May God's Spirit be upon you as you lead your class on their *Journey Through the Bible*!

Questions or comments?
Call Curric-U-Phone 1-800-251-8591.

1

Mark 1:21-28

THE KINGDOM OF GOD HAS COME NEAR

LEARNING MENU

Keeping in mind the ways in which your class members learn best as well as their needs and interests, choose at least one learning segment from each of the three Dimensions that follow. Remember that Dimension 1 activities explore what the Bible says and put biblical events into a larger geographical and historical context. Dimension 2 activities explore what Jesus meant according to the writer of the Book of Mark and how Mark's original readers and hearers heard it. Dimension 3 activities explore what the passages mean in students' personal lives, congregational lives, and lives as disciples in God's world.

One theme that emerges from Mark 1:21-28 is Jesus' access to the power of God. Prayer vividly connects us with the living God and shapes the context in which the church studies and understands Scripture. Therefore, each session includes an opening and closing prayer. Use them as part of your personal meditation and preparation to teach. Adapt them and use them with your class.

Opening Prayer
Creating, Redeeming, Sustaining God, we know that you are ever near and loving us. Yet you are also ever mysterious to us. So, we gather together as your people to begin a new study of your ways and your purpose for us. Open our hearts and our minds to your word. Give us courage to risk asking the questions we have. Give us tolerance for one another's ideas, for we all are seeking to know you. Strengthen our faith in you as we seek further insights into Mark's story of Jesus. All this we ask in the name of the Christ. Amen.

Introduce your students to the Gospel of Mark. Invite them to begin a conversation with some of that book's theological concerns, within the framework of their larger journey through the Bible as a whole. Open the dialogue by helping students explore the origins of Mark, what the first chapter says to us about Mark's intentions, and what the first chapter says about Jesus' ministry and message.

Exploring facts and meanings then and now are all necessary to help us mature in our journey of faith.

Dimension 1:
What Does the Bible Say?

- Divide your class into three groups as members arrive in the classroom. Have one group work on the map, one on the timeline, and one on the video.
- As the groups finish, invite them to come together and briefly share one or two insights about Jesus or the Book of Mark.

(A) Map Jesus' journey.

- Before class hang up a map of Palestine in New Testament times, preferably one that shows Palestine in relation to Africa. The *Bible Teacher Kit* includes several helpful maps.
- Have a ball of yarn and pins available. As students arrive, invite them to work together to identify the places mentioned in Mark 1.
- Start the yarn at Nazareth and tack it down at the places where Jesus went. Do not cut the yarn (leave it dangling); students will track Jesus' journey each week.

TEACHING TIP

Adults learn better by doing something with data, rather than just looking at a map, so get them involved in searching the Bible for the steps of Jesus' journey. Have a globe available for them to locate modern Palestine.

(B) Build a timeline.

- Have students build their own timeline on the wall of your classroom. Leave it up all quarter if you can. This activity will help students visually place the historical time of Jesus (and of the Book of Mark) into a much larger time frame.
- Before class tack up a long brightly colored string or yarn that stretches the length of one wall.
- At the far right side place a sign with the current year. Prepare two sets of 3-by-5 index cards (events in one color; dates in another color):

Earth begins	4500 million years ago
Mammals emerged	80 million years ago
Human-types emerged	4-5 million years ago
Homo Sapiens emerged	100,000-200,000 years ago
Pottery invented	7,500 years ago (5500 B.C.)
Picture writing began	5,500 years ago (3500 B.C.)
Old Testament times	4,000-2,500 years ago
Great Wall of China built	400 B.C.—A.D. 1600
Mayan civilization peaked in Central America	A.D. 250-600
Jesus' ministry begins	1,968+ years ago (A.D. 26)
Jesus crucified	1,965+ years ago (A.D. 29)

Book of Mark written	1,930 years ago (A.D. 60's)
Plymouth Colony settled	A.D. 1620
Birth of the U.S.A.	A.D. 1776
First TV program broadcast by NBC	A.D. 1939
First human in space (Russia/Yuri Gagarin)	A.D. 1961

- Give both sets of cards to early arriving students to match and then to place on the timeline (dates below; events above). Use masking tape to wall mount. Let students struggle a little to make guesses before sharing the correct matches.
- Invite students to make additional cards about other events they know.
- For example, do your students know approximate dates of the Stone Age, Copper Age, Bronze Age, Iron Age? dates of dinosaur life and the Ice Age? dates of the Anasazi (ancient ancestors of current Native American peoples)? dates when peoples moved from hunters/gatherers to farming to the industrial revolution? dates of movement from tribes to city-states to empires? The point of this activity is to help class members gain a "telescopic and wide-lens picture" within which God's amazing action happened in the life, death, and resurrection of Jesus.
- In a brief discussion of this activity, point out that the writer of Mark quickly provided a historical context for his readers by grounding Jesus' activity in the traditions of the Hebrew religion. (See study book, page 7) Jesus, according to Mark, must be understood as a bridge connecting Jewish tradition and God's stunningly new word/action for the world. From our late twentieth century position, as we take an even longer look back, we too need that context—and a broader one. We can only marvel anew at God's action in speaking through a carpenter from Nazareth in Galilee at that time in our earth's life in a land dominated and controlled by Roman outsiders!

(C) View a video about Northern Palestine.

- Show Part One of the video in the *Bible Teaching Kit*, which offers a view of northern Palestine that includes Galilee where Jesus was born and where he began his ministry at age thirty.
- Invite students to jot down three or four interesting facts about Jesus' homeland while they view this portion of the video.

—Have you considered the influence of African cultures upon Palestine?

(D) Review questions in the study book.

- The answers to Dimension 1 questions can be discovered by reading Mark 1:1-45.
- If students have not read the passage before class, give them time when they arrive to read the passage and write out answers to the questions.
- Review the sequence of the story and the answers to the questions with the class.
- Urge members in following weeks to read the assigned passages in their Bibles and consider the questions in their books before coming to class. Reading the passage and getting it clearly in mind lays the groundwork for the class to explore the more theological questions that the writer of the study book raises in Dimension 2.

Dimension 2: What Does the Bible Mean?

(E) Discuss John the Baptizer.

The following discussion questions will help you and your class explore the material offered in the study book about John the Baptizer and Jesus' baptism.

- Pose the questions and let students venture their own theories before sharing ideas from below or from the study book. Be careful not to jump to the twentieth century in your interpretation here! Stay with the text and your exploration of what the writer of Mark was probably saying to his original readers!
—Why do you think that the writer of Mark began with the story of John the Baptizer?
—What is the writer of Mark really trying to tell his readers about Jesus?
—How does the story of John the Baptizer help him tell it?
- Mark's quotation of the Old Testament verses at the beginning of his Gospel were meant to tell his readers that they cannot understand Jesus without understanding his relationship to the Hebrew Bible. The story of John signals the specific fulfillment of those Old Testament passages. The story also signals to Mark's original readers that everything that follows about Jesus is, according to Mark, to be seen as the fulfillment of all God's dealings with Israel.
- In these first thirteen verses we have Mark's christological statement. As the author of the study book notes, Jesus' arrival on the scene constitutes "a decisive, climactic shift within human history" (study book, page 7).
- A look again at the timeline done in activity (B) confirms visually one impact of that shift, since we have come to identify historical time as "before Christ" (B.C.)

or "before the common era" (B.C.E.) and "after date" or "in the year of our Lord" (A.D.) or "the common era" (C.E.).

(F) Explore the meaning of Jesus' exorcism.

- Answer the following questions:
—How do scholars look at Mark's story of Jesus casting out the demon in Mark 1:21-28?
—Why did only the unclean spirit recognize Jesus?
—Why did the bystanders call the exorcism "a new teaching"? (Mark 1:27)
—As Mark tells this story, did Jesus stand within the structures of his religious tradition? Did he move beyond that tradition in any respect?
- If your class is large, divide it into two or three groups. Provide a copy (for each group) of the background article, "On the Meaning of Mark 1:21–28," page 7.
- When the class has finished its research, ask members to share insights about the passage.
  Evidently the unclean spirit knew who Jesus was because he recognized in Jesus the divine power to destroy him. Mark may have told the story this way to underscore his point that the power by which Jesus healed and the authority with which Jesus taught are one and the same.
- Jesus honored the Jewish sabbath and worked within the synagogue. Yet he was perceived as one whose authority transcended that of the scribes (who were the trained biblical scholars of Jesus' day). As Mark's story continues we will see this controversy build between Jesus and the scribes.
- Questions 2 and 3 infer that much in Mark's Gospel is surprising, offbeat, or elliptical. Frequently Mark teases the reader's thought without always giving clear answers. When first-time readers of this Gospel become aware that this was one of the author's preferred techniques for telling the story of Jesus, its frustrations are somewhat more bearable, if not softened.
- Question 4 picks up a basic theme that runs throughout not only Mark's Gospel but most of the Bible. All of the Gospels, Paul's letters, and the Old Testament's prophetic literature—to select only three ready examples—develop the theme that God worked within the covenant community's history while at the same time summoning that community to new insights and responsibilities.

(G) Explore the exorcism and the good news together.

—Lead the class to look at Mark 1:14-15 and Mark 1:21-28 together.

—What does the writer of Mark seem to be telling his readers by placing these two stories near each other?

—That is, what is the relationship between these two events of Jesus' preaching and Jesus' casting out the demon?

- The questions posed in this activity presuppose that passages from Mark cannot be fully understood unless they are read in connection with each other and with the overall context of the Gospel. This is a cardinal principle of all modern interpretation of the Bible.

- Mark implied (as he continued to do throughout the book) that the power of the kingdom of God is to be heard and seen—in word and deed—by those who have ears and eyes. Jesus gathered up the old and inaugurated the new in his words and his deeds. The expulsion of demonic forces signaled to the original readers that God's power (kingdom) was sweeping into human history.

Dimension 3:
What Does the Bible Mean to Us?

(H) Write about evil and good news today.

- Briefly remind students of the points made in Dimension 3 of their study book: the text is not us; none of it was first written with us in mind; the differences between the world of Bible times does not have to mean either abandoning the Bible or our intellect; we can learn from those differences something important for our own lives in the twentieth century. Remind them that the writer of Mark used the common image of a person with unclean spirit(s) or demons within them to portray evil forces in his day. Then ask individuals to write their own thoughts on these questions:

—How would I symbolize "evil" in today's world?

—How would I state the "good news" of God's power for today's world?

- Allow time for writing answers in a journal. Then ask one or two people to share briefly their images of evil and their statements of good news. Conclude this activity by having individuals write in their journal any questions they still have about what Jesus was saying or about what Mark was trying to tell his readers about Jesus through this first chapter of the Book of Mark.

TEACHING TIP

Encourage students to place these writings in a journal that they then bring each week to use for other "journaling activities." (Loose paper in a filing folder is fine.)

(I) Explore theological issues.

- Divide the class into two groups.
- Ask one group to discuss the question: What does Mark 1:21-28 tell us about Jesus?
- Ask the other group to discuss the question: What does Mark 1:21-28 tell us about human beings?
- After about ten minutes of discussion in the smaller groups, call the class back together. Invite students' reflections. List their responses on chalkboard or newsprint in two columns. *(Possible answers might be some of the following: Jesus healed and taught within the structures of his Jewish religious tradition; Jesus exerted God-given authority over dehumanizing forces; Jesus was recognized as God's Holy One by a demoniac—by one whose utterances might have been dismissed as deluded or crazy; human beings in this passage show themselves to be religious and receptive to learn, subject to possession by "unclean spirits" even in a religious setting, astounded by Jesus but not necessarily perceptive about who Jesus is.)*
- Encourage students to relate their answers to the two questions. That is, ask them to ponder the relationship, suggested by Mark, between human beings and God as we know God through Jesus of Nazareth. *(Possible responses might include the following: human beings seek God through religious institutions such as synagogue, church, or Scripture, and God is pleased to meet them there; or God wills the healing of women and men from debilitating forces, even those that sometimes exist within religious contexts; or there is more to Jesus and to God than meets the mortal eye; or paradoxically, Jesus is well known, yet not known well by the masses.)*

(J) Explore the way of discipleship.

- Dimension 3 material in the study book poses a challenging question about accepting authority (along with the first followers of Jesus) from a Christ who wielded a balanced kind of authority, a Christ who wove the strengths of tradition with the questions and challenges of bold new ideas and ways of being and living with each other.
- Ask class members to turn to a neighbor and explore the question of what it might mean in today's world to invoke that same kind of balanced, dynamic authority in our congregation; in our denomination; in the world at large. Caution dyads to be sure that both partners get a chance to talk. End this activity by having a few people share a new insight gained from their conversation.

(K) Sing Scripture.

- Provide newsprint, markers, and hymnals with the hymn "When Jesus Came to Jordan" (*The United*

Methodist Hymnal, No. 252) or another hymn based on Mark 1:9-11.

- Sing the hymn. Compare the words of the hymn with the Scripture from Mark.
- Answer the following questions:
—Does the hymn portray the sense of the Scripture accurately?
—How would you change the hymn words to convey the idea today?
- Just before the closing prayer, sing the hymn again with any words, verses, or phrases you have created.
- Do the same activity with the other hymns. Divide the class into two or three teams. Hymn possibilities may include "Tú Has Venido a la Orilla" ("Lord, You Have Come to the Lakeshore") (*The United Methodist Hymnal*, No. 344). This hymn portrays Mark 1:16-20, the calling of the disciples and us. Or "Silence, Frenzied, Unclean Spirit" (No. 264), which is based on Mark 1:21-28, the casting out of the demon.

Dimension 4:
A Daily Bible Journey Plan

- Discuss with the class the purpose of this Bible journey plan: to help those who wish to read through the complete Bible while they are engaged in the sixteen-volume JOURNEY THROUGH THE BIBLE series. Encourage class members to read this week the suggested selections for chapters 1 and 2 of this volume in order to catch up.
- Invite class members who wish to do so to memorize Jesus' message in Mark 1:15, which is in effect a summary of Jesus' message throughout the Gospel of Mark.
- Invite students to write out answers to the questions in chapter 2 before coming to the next class. If you will choose journaling activities throughout the study, remind students to bring a notebook to each session for journaling and reflection activities.

Closing Prayer
Gracious God, we are thankful to be together on this journey through the Bible. To the best of our ability, we offer you our open minds and our receiving hearts as we reach back across the centuries to a world different from ours, and yet with many similarities of evil forces. With your help, we have begun to open our hearts and minds anew to Mark's gospel story of Jesus' ministry and his message of your love and your power. Amen.

Additional Bible Helps

On the Meaning of Mark 1:21-28
Let us candidly admit that Mark 1:21-28 is a difficult text in many respects. Briefly told, it makes jumps in thought that are unclear and assumes the reality of demon exorcism, something difficult for many modern readers to grasp. In all these respects this story is representative of the entire Gospel. Mark 1:21-28 offers us a threshold into a different world.

This passage raises fundamental questions about life as viewed from the vantage point of Christian faith—that is, questions about God, human beings, and the relationship between God and human beings.

If we get entangled in barren questions of bare fact—"Are there such things as demons?" or "What procedure did Jesus use to cast them out?"—we shall probably end up (1) frustrated by unanswerable questions, (2) upset with those Christians whose answers differ from our own, and (3) distracted from the issues for faith with which Mark was profoundly concerned.

Therefore, in dealing with this text about an exorcism at Capernaum, bear in mind that Mark has practically no interest in explaining *how* it happened. Mark is inviting us to ponder what it means that Jesus exercised power over demonic forces. The writer of the Book of Mark, in other words, is inviting us to think theologically.
—By Clifton Black

2

Mark 2:1-19a

WE HAVE NEVER SEEN ANYTHING LIKE THIS!

LEARNING MENU

Keeping in mind the ways in which your class members learn best as well as their needs and interests, choose at least one learning segment from each of the three Dimensions that follow. Remember that Dimension 1 activities explore what the Bible says and put biblical events into a larger geographical and historical context. Dimension 2 activities explore what Jesus meant according to the writer of the Book of Mark and how Mark's original readers and hearers heard it. Dimension 3 activities explore what the passages mean in students' personal lives, congregational lives, and lives as disciples in God's world.

To get students deeply involved with the biblical story rather than just learning about it, use one form of the picture study/roleplay in Dimension 3.

Opening Prayer
Amazing God, you who are ever near to us and ever pursuing us with your love and forgiveness, we open our hearts and our minds to you. Speak to us through the words of Mark and through the story he tells of your amazing work in your son Jesus. We seek to know more about him. We seek to take his story of your love into our hearts. We seek to become more faithful disciples of Jesus, whom we know as the Christ. In the name of Jesus we pray, Amen.

Dimension 1:
What Does the Bible Say?

Activities A, B, and C can be offered as choices as students first arrive in the classroom.

(A) Map Jesus' journey.

- As students arrive, have them work on the wall map they began last time. The places mentioned in this week's passages include Capernaum, Sea of Galilee, Levi's house in Capernaum, back to the Sea of Galilee, and the mountains. Some events take place at unknown places. A few moments of reflection on the map journey so far can elicit from the students the facts that
- Mark has Jesus moving around a lot!
- Mark wasn't particularly interested in giving his readers all the specific details about Jesus'whereabouts.
- For further reflection, ask how many years Jesus was engaged in his ministry. *(It was about three years from his baptism by John to his crucifixion in Jerusalem.)* We can see that three years of Jesus' life is condensed into a set of stories that Mark has selected to make the points for his own purposes.

(B) Get the big picture of Mark.

- Before class prepare the five title sheets needed for this activity. Print one title with its number on each sheet of paper:
  - I.   The Beginnings of Jesus' Ministry
  - II. The Galilean Ministry: North of Palestine
  - III. Ministry on the Journey to Judea: South Palestine
  - IV. The Last Week of Jesus' Life
  - V.   After the Crucifixion
- Working together with their Bibles, ask students to pick out the major events that Mark tells about and print each event on a blank index card. (Have plenty of cards available.) Arrange these event cards under the appropriate title sheets to form an overall "big picture" of the events that Mark describes as he tries to help his readers know who Jesus is. These might be laid out on a table like a board game or tacked onto a bulletin board.
- Speculate with students about why Mark included the "healing" or "miracle" stories. Also speculate on why Mark tells a number of stories about Jesus' responses to the scribes or Pharisees.
- An alternate way to do this activity: If you have less time in class, prepare the small event cards ahead of time. Pick out the major passages in each week's lessons and print one event on each card. Students then can place the event cards under the five title sheets. Encourage use of Bibles.

TEACHING TIP
Don't try to include every event; rather, encourage students to select the main events. The point of this activity is to help students learn the five phases of Mark's Gospel.

(C) Review questions in the study book.

Review the questions students have answered in chapter two of their study books. Answers to Dimension 1 questions are as follows:

1. Jesus' reason for forgiving the man's sins was that he saw the faith of the paralytic's friends.

2. Jesus recognized their faith by their action in bringing the man to Jesus to be healed (Mark 2:5a).

3. Jesus first forgave the man's sins (Mark 2:5b).

4. The scribes responded with "Why does this fellow speak this way? It is blasphemy! Who can forgive sins but God alone?" (Mark 2:7)

5. Jesus told the man to get up and go home in order to show the scribes that he (the Son of man) had authority on earth to forgive sins (Mark 2:10).

Once you have clarified what the Bible says move to activity (D) in Dimension 2 to explore what Jesus meant by his sayings in these stories and why the writer of Mark told these passages to his readers.

Dimension 2: What Does the Bible Mean?

(D) Explore meanings.

- Use the following discussion questions to explore the entire passage of Mark assigned for this session (Mark 2:1-19a).
—Why did Jesus first respond to the paralytic by claiming that his sins were forgiven?
—On what basis did the scribes conclude that Jesus' pronouncement of the paralytic's forgiveness was blasphemous?
—Which was easier to say to the paralytic, "Your sins are forgiven" or "Stand up, take up your mat, and go home"?
—What is the common element that "glues together" the stories in Mark 2:1—3:6? What message is Mark proclaiming by grouping these stories together?
—When Mark says that Jesus saw the faith of the paralytic's friends, what does Mark mean by *faith*?
—Mark's stories of Jesus, and in fact, Jesus' original actions and thus God's surprising acts of grace, prompted amazement from the onlookers. Is this faith? Why or why not? What is it ultimately that Mark was trying to tell his readers about Jesus, about God, about faith?

These six questions in one way or another all support the same general conclusion. In the Book of Mark things are not always what they seem to be! Surprises abound! Jesus forgives sins when the man and his friends expect a physical healing. The crowd is astounded, but does not really understand. Their culture prepares them for a hero, a wonder worker. Their religion leads them to expect a king, a messiah. The scribes, the trained scholars of the day, seem to miss the point!

TEACHING TIP
Keep students focused on discovering what Jesus was saying to his *original* hearers—and what the writer of Mark was saying to his *original* readers or listeners. "Walk around inside the passages" to discover what they probably meant "back then." When we get to Dimension 3 activities, we may discover the passages mean much the same to us today, or we may discover that from our twentieth century stance, we hear God speaking through those passages to us in a different way. In any case, hold the "meaning for us now" discussions until later!

(E) Research *Son of Man*.

- Pose the question, What do scholars think the phrase "Son of Man" meant in Mark 2:10?

- Provide students with resources such as the NRSV Bible; commentaries such as *The Gospel According to Saint Mark*, by Morna Hooker, pages 87-93; *The Good News According to Mark*, by Eduard Schweizer, page 59; *Harper's Bible Commentary*, pages 988 and 994; and Bible dictionaries. Remind students to look at the sidebar in their study book, page 16. Also share with them information found in the article, "Son of Man," found in the Additional Bible Helps section at the end of this session.

- Ask students to work in small groups (or in subgroups of three or four members) to find out what scholars think the phrase meant. Encourage them to look up some of the biblical references scholars note for the different meanings of the phrase. Give the class sufficient time to read, take some notes, and formulate a brief report on their findings. Then call them together to hear the reports. Jot a word or phrase on a chalkboard for each different meaning or theory that scholars offer. What seems to be the predominant view of biblical scholars today?

TEACHING TIP

While the initial answer to this question is nicely summarized in the study book, page 16, the point of this activity is to help students get underneath that summary to see where the writer of the study book was getting his information to write this summary. This activity provides a way for students to get used to "poking around" in commentaries and dictionaries to see what different biblical scholars think and say.

- An alternate way to do this activity: If you don't want to use the time in class for the research, ask students at the end of session 1 to take the various resource books home and come back to this second session with their mini-reports.

Reflection on the mini-reports after they have been given in class should include some discussion of the fact that "things are not always what they seem." What Jesus meant may be somewhat ambiguous and mysterious.

Dimension 3:
What Does the Bible Mean to Us?

(F) Do a picture study and find personal meanings.

- Find a large teaching picture (preferably in color) of the story of the paralytic being healed—or perhaps more than one picture that portrays different phases in the story. Stand or hang these in the classroom together so that class members may sit and study them. (A good source for teaching pictures is children's curriculum. Many churches keep pictures on file.)

- Tell the class that you are going to guide them in meditating on the picture(s) for a few minutes. Use the following words to guide the meditation. Read them slowly and meditatively. Wherever you come to a series of ellipses (. . .), pause to let class members think and feel in silence. *Go very slowly!*

  Take a minute to get comfortable in your chair and to be sure you can see the picture(s). . . . Breathe in and out slowly while you look at the different people in the picture(s). . . . Does your eye stop on one of the people? Notice Jesus. . . . Now let your eyes wander over the other people. . . . Which one other than Jesus catches your eye? . . . Perhaps it is someone in the crowd inside or in the doorway or on the street outside. . . . Perhaps you find yourself looking back again at one of the people carrying the paralyzed one . . . or perhaps your eye is caught by the paralyzed person . . . or perhaps you are looking at one of the scribes in the crowd who came to check Jesus out. . . . Whichever person catches your eye, look at that person long and carefully . . . (longer pause/silence). . . . Try to feel your way inside that person's being. . . . What might he or she be feeling? . . . Where did he or she come from that day? . . . Why is she or he there in that crowd? . . . Can you feel into that person? . . . Try to take on that person's life for a moment. . . . Why are you there? . . . What have you heard about this man Jesus? . . . What do you hope for? . . . What do you think as you hear Jesus offer words of forgiveness? . . . What do you feel when Jesus says "stand up and go home"? . . . What do you say to those who are next to you? . . . What do you hear them saying? . . . (longer pause) . . . Now begin to come slowly back into the twentieth century . . . back into this classroom. . . .

- Allow members to sit a minute in silence, then give them a choice of the following activities:

—Have them write in their journals about the person in the picture and about any insights they have gained about what the "good news" is. They might try to create their own title to the story they just experienced.

—Have them express artistically with materials provided at an art table their feelings and insights about the person they "became." (Provide large sheets of white drawing paper, water color paints, and chalk, crayons, or felt-tip markers.) Encourage expression with lines, shapes, or swirls of color rather than with realistic drawings.

(G) Create a still-life picture.

- Ask the class to form a still-life group picture by assuming a pose that would reflect the beginning of the story. (That is, designate one area of the room as the house, note where the door is and where the road is; then ask people to place themselves into the picture and "freeze.") Be sure different people take the roles of the paralytic, his friends, Jesus, the scribes, the crowd.
- Tell the story as dramatically as possible (or read it expressively and dramatically). After verse 4, say to the class, "Re-form the picture as it develops." Then continue telling the story through verse 11. Stop again and say "Re-form the picture as it is now. Use your face and bodies to show what you're thinking and feeling."
- Finish the story, then ask the class to relax.
- Gather the class back together. Ask:
- —How do you feel about being in the picture?
- —What did the story mean to you personally? (Let people share personal meanings for as much time as you have allotted.)

(H) Roleplay the story.

- Ask people to assume the various roles in the story. Be sure to include Jesus, scribes, paralytic, his four friends (some of whom might be women), and people in the crowd.
- Give them time to reread the story and refresh their memory about their particular character—how do they think he or she felt and acted; what did they say? Encourage those in the crowd to determine what they will say to those who are standing next to them.
- Set the stage by telling the class which part of the room is the house, where the door is, and where the road and the steps to the roof are.
- Ask them to assume their places for the beginning of the story. Tell them to freeze and assume their character. Then say "Let the story begin." When the story is finished, gather the class together again and use the same discussion questions listed in activity (G).

- If you have time, you might conclude this roleplay and discussion by having people write in their journals or do the art activity. But try to leave time in your lesson plan for the next activity, which moves persons from personal meanings to exploring meanings of corporate discipleship.

(I) Dig deeper for discipleship meanings.

- As a mini-lecture, relate the information on faith found in the article, "Faith as a Word-Deed." (See the Additional Bible Helps section at the end of this chapter.) Add your own ideas or examples about faith as action.
- Ask the following questions:
- —What is the message about faith for us in the twentieth century?
- —If faith is a word-deed, how do we "faith" in relation to the poor, the homeless, the gay and lesbian community, those whose religious beliefs are different from ours, those whose race or ethnic backgrounds are different from our own?
- —If we act our faith in Jesus, what might we do differently as a local congregation?
- —If the whole church were to act its faith in Jesus, what might the church-at-large do differently in the world?

Closing Prayer

O loving One, you come to us in surprising ways! May we always be open in heart and mind for your stunningly fresh word and deed. We love the old, old story of Jesus and how he tells us of your love. Help us always to be open to deeper and deeper meanings of that most special story. We have struggled to understand what Jesus meant by faith. We have looked anew at how his very life modeled faith as your divine word-in-action. We have looked within to see how we too might go into your world being your word-in-action. Help us as we continue to live as Jesus' disciples in our world today. All this we ask in the name of the Christ, your beloved Son. Amen.

Additional Bible Helps

Son of Man

Biblical scholar Morna Hooker notes that in Mark the phrase, "Son of Man," is used fourteen times. Mark has Jesus openly using the phrase to refer to himself. Therefore, notes Hooker, the phrase in Mark is not part of the secret identity of Jesus as the Messiah (page 89).

If Jesus was not referring to himself as the Messiah by the use of that phrase, then was he simply referring to himself as a human being? Dr. Hooker notes that some scholars believe he was. The phrase "Son of Man" (Mark

2:10) is the result of a misunderstanding in translation and refers to "human being" in general. Dr. Hooker, however, finds that explanation unsatisfactory, noting that "for Jesus to claim that man [as human being] has the power to forgive sin would certainly justify the charge of blasphemy" (page 87). Nor does such an explanation adequately account for Jesus' power to heal as related to forgiveness of sins.

Hooker raises basic questions about this phrase "Son of Man" as Mark used it: Was it possible for Jesus to use the phrase "the Son of Man" as a way of referring to himself (as Mark implies)? And why would Jesus have done so? More specifically, why does the phrase seem to refer specifically to Jesus' mission? (page 92). Hooker summarizes research on question one (see pages 88-93). Then she notes that scholarly evidence supports the conclusion that the original Aramaic phrase that Mark translates literally into Greek could be used by a speaker to refer to himself or herself. Therefore, Jesus probably did use it to refer to himself.

In responding to the second question of why Jesus used it or how Jesus meant the phrase to be heard, Hooker notes that Jesus was probably applying to himself the imagery of Daniel 7 and Ezekiel, an imagery that would have been familiar to his Jewish listeners. Says Hooker, "The phrase was by no means a colourless way of referring to oneself: it conjured up all kinds of associations: the prophetic call-ing; the mission of God's obedient people; the possibility of suffering for those who were faithful to his will; the promise of final vindication" (pages 92-93). Hooker suggests that Jesus used the phrase "not as a title, not because he was claiming to 'be' the messianic Son of man, but because he accepted for himself the role of obedient faith which the term evokes, and because he called others to share that calling with him" (page 93).

From *The Gospel According to Saint Mark*, by Morna D. Hooker, Black's New Testament Commentary Series (Hendrickson, 1991; pages 87-93).

Faith as a Word-Deed

Faith—what is it? Mark wants us to understand that for Jesus, faith was not a matter of saying, "I believe in Jesus." It wasn't a matter of believing that Jesus was a miracle worker, a kind of super-hero. Faith wasn't a matter of keeping all the laws of the Jewish religion. No, Jesus was portraying something else about God and God's ways. Jesus was portraying something about God's expectations about faith in people. Jesus was saying that faith involves action. We usually consider faith to be a noun. But, actually for Jesus faith is almost a verb! It is a word-deed.

Jesus actually demonstrated this combination noun-verb by forgiving the paralytic's sins (authoritative word) and healing his paralysis (healing deed). Furthermore, the paralytic's faith was an action: he went to Jesus to be healed.

3

Mark 4:1-20

ᴍANY THINGS IN PARABLES

LEARNING MENU

Again, keep in mind your class of learners and how they best learn. But surprise them a little too—and they may well surprise you! If you discover students are not reading the passage in their Bible and writing out answers to the Dimension 1 questions at home before class, suggest that they read the passage and answer the questions when they first come into the classroom. Other activities might be offered to arriving students who have already completed the questions. In this session activities (A) and (B) would be good to offer as students are first arriving. Activity (B) from the last session in "The Big Picture of Mark" might be offered again if only a few had a chance to work on it.

Opening Prayer

O God, you are the creator, redeemer, and sustainer of all of life! You are ever dependable and yet always surprising us anew! Give us courage to open our hearts to your surprising ways. Help us to risk loosening our hold on our traditional ways of looking at your word that we might be open to the possibility of a new word from you who are the living God. Open our ears and our hearts to the living word in the parables Jesus taught. Keep us growing in our faith in you as we continue to learn anew about your Son Jesus and about what faith and discipleship are. In Jesus' name we pray. Amen.

Dimension 1:
What Does the Bible Say?

(A) Explore parallel Gospels.

- Look up the parable of the sower in Matthew 13:18-23; Luke 8:11-15 and Mark 4:3-20. Find out how similar or different they are.
- Read not only the parable itself but also Jesus' explanation that follows.
- Share with the students information from the article, "What Is the Synoptic Problem?" found on page 17.

TEACHING TIP
One way for students to compare Gospels is for one person to read the Mark passage and another to follow in reading the Matthew and Luke parallels. When differences are found, stop and discuss them.

(B) Continue mapping Jesus' journey.

- Invite students to continue tracking the travels of Jesus during his three-year ministry. In the last session we left Jesus on the mountain. Today, beginning with Mark 3:19b Jesus "goes home" (probably Nazareth), then back to the Sea of Galilee (4:1), probably the west side of the sea (which we surmise from the later context in 4:35 and 5:1).

- Read about the Sea of Galilee and Nazareth in a Bible dictionary.

(C) Review questions in the study book.

- Review the answers to the questions in the study book for this session.

1. The four situations in which the seed is sown and what happened to the seed are: (a) it fell on the path—birds ate it; (b) it fell on rocky ground—it was scorched by the sun and withered because it had no depth of soil; (c) it fell among thorns—it grew but was choked by the thorns so that it could not yield any grain; (d) it fell on good soil—the seed grew and brought forth grain, yielding 30 and 60 and 100 times more than the original seed.

2. Mark said that Jesus told parables in order that they might look, but not really see; listen, but not really hear. Further he said that they failed to see and hear in order that they might not turn again to God and be forgiven. Mark said Jesus was quoting from Isaiah 6:9-10 as a way to note that some people are among the "elect" and others are "outsiders." We will think more about this in activity (E) and (H) and question 4.

3. The seed was "the word" (Mark 4:14).

Dimension 2: What Does the Bible Mean?

(D) Talk about parables.

- Give information to students found in the section "Jesus Teaches" found in Additional Bible Helps, page 17.
- Ask the class to share their understandings about how Jesus taught his first listeners.

(E) Explore meanings of *sower*.

The following discussion questions may help you and your students understand Jesus' explanation of the parable of the sower and Mark's intent in sharing it with his first readers/listeners. Initial answers and understandings may be found in the Dimension 2 material of the study book. Remind students that the introduction to this session in their study book talks about "many things in parables" and the possibility that we might not entirely understand!

- Discuss the following:
—What is a parable?

—Begin this discussion by reviewing what a parable is and is not (see the article in the study book, pages 21-22).

—What, do you think, did Jesus mean to convey to his listeners by telling the parable of the sower?

Some scholars note that in 4:2 there is no hint that Jesus himself was trying to obscure the meaning of his teachings. The obscurity may come from Mark, who was writing at a little later time, and from the point of faith in the risen Christ. The key to what Mark seems to be saying is found in 4:13, where he suggested that this parable was not only a key to Jesus' teaching, but a key to Jesus' whole ministry. Mark probably intended for his readers to be confronted with the story of Jesus. Those who hear and respond will have the secret of the kingdom of God; those who do not hear and repond are the ones whose hearts are hardened.

The word *listen* at the beginning of the parable itself (4:3), says biblical scholar Morna Hooker, "is derived from a Hebrew verb which means not only 'to listen' and 'to hear' (4:9), but also 'to obey,' and thus implies an active response to what is heard" (*The Gospel According to Saint Mark*, page 122).

—How is Jesus' parable about the kingdom of God different from what an apocalyptist in Jesus' day might have said about the Kingdom?

- Plan ahead and seek permission to photocopy the article "Apocalyptic Literature: Mystery With Meaning" from the *Bible Teacher Kit*, pages 71-74 (write Cokesbury, Syndications—Permissions Office, P.O. Box 801, Nashville, TN 37202). Then provide students with copies of this article as well as "On the Meaning of the Kingdom of God" in the section on Additional Bible Helps at the end of this session, page 17.
- Have members work in pairs to discover how an apocalyptic meaning of Kingdom differs from a view of the kingdom as both here and not yet here within human historical time.
- After teams of two have worked awhile, invite them to join into teams of four and share their learnings with each other. Invite them to report back to the whole class with major insights and learnings.

—What reason did Mark give in Mark 4:10-12 for Jesus' telling parables instead of speaking plainly? Why did Mark give this reason to his readers?

- If students did activity (A) earlier, invite them to apply what they learned in that activity to this question.

—What differences did they discern in the intent of the Gospel writers?

—Why might have Mark used the technique of disguising the meanings of what Jesus taught?

(F) Experience the parable through your senses.

This activity invites students to take in the parable with all their senses as you prepare them and then read it to them.

- Ask students to settle comfortably in their chairs for a guided reflection time. Use the following words to get them into a reflective state. Remember, the ellipses (. . .) represent a pause to let students feel and reflect on what you have said.
- Be prepared to read Mark 4:3-8 at the end of these preparation words.

> *Relax and make yourself very comfortable ... . Take a few slow even breaths... . Close your eyes if you wish ... . Imagine that you are in the crowd by the Sea of Galilee where Jesus is teaching... . Notice where the water's edge is... . Notice the rolling hills on which you sit, ... the steep cliffs across the water... . Feel the fresh breezes from the water... . Smell the fish ... . Can you almost taste them?... Listen to the birds ... . Feel the warm sun on you . . . . What other smells are there?... What other sounds do you hear close by?... What sounds come from farther away?... Can you feel the touches, the gentle bumps of others who are close around you?... What textures do you feel from their clothing?... Oh, look!... Jesus is beginning to speak again.* (Read the parable here without mentioning the chapter and verse numbers. Read it very expressively as if Jesus were telling it to a large crowd. When you have finished reading it, pause and then continue with the following words.)

> *Listen. It is so quiet I can hear the sea ... . Now people around me are beginning to stir, beginning to talk to each other again (long pause) ... . When you are ready, slowly bring yourself back into the twentieth century and back into our classroom ... .*

- Use reflection questions after this activity:
—How did it feel to try to take in the setting for the parable with all your senses?
—Share some of the sounds, sights, smells, tastes, and touches you experienced sitting by the sea.
—As you listened to the parable itself, what did you experience? Did you sense any special sounds, sights, smells, tastes, or touches related to the ground, the seed, the birds, the sun, and so forth?
—What sense did you make of the parable as you imagined "sitting by the sea listening to Jesus"?

TEACHING TIP

The temptation will be to leap immediately to what it means to us today in the twentieth century, but try to keep students focused for a little while on their imagined experiences in the first century. The purpose of this activity is to help students gain insights about probable meanings "back then."

Dimension 3: What Does the Bible Mean to Us?

(G) Create a modern parable.

- Create a modern day setting and story that might reveal Jesus' understanding of the nature of the kingdom of God. (Jesus used the setting and image of a field and a farmer sowing seed—an image and experience that was common and very much a part of his original listeners' first century experience.)
—What kind of setting and story might Jesus use today to tell twentieth century listeners about the kingdom of God?
—How will the story portray differences from what modern day Pharisees teach about the Kingdom?
—How will the story's message about the Kingdom be different from what modern day apocalyptists preach?
—Reread the article on "Parables" in the study book pages 21-22, to increase your understanding about parables.

(H) Discuss outsiders and insiders.

This activity would be a good follow-up to activity (E) in Dimension 2.
- Invite the class to explore who might be considered "insiders" and "outsiders" today and why. To answer this question, members will need to remember and consider what kind of response Jesus seemed to require of a disciple: faith as word-deed.

(I) Explore the meaning of faith and discipleship.

Discuss the following questions as a class:
—What does all that we have read, and felt, and heard, and thought in this class session seem to say to us about what faith really is? About what discipleship involves?
—What might we conclude about what the church today should offer as its message about God and Jesus? What kind of evangelism and outreach is implied? What kind of justice mission is implied?

(J) Keep a journal on discipleship.

As a closing activity, ask students to take a few minutes to write their thoughts and feelings on how they might need to change their lives if they begin to take the message of Mark about Jesus and God's kingdom more seriously. After giving people time to write, close with a prayer.

Dimension 4:
A Daily Bible Journey Plan

Mark 4:21-25 contains four separate sayings, which Mark has grouped together. We are not clear to whom Jesus was speaking in 4:21 (the disciples? the crowd?) By grouping the sayings together, with two more commands (in 4:23-24a) to listen and hear, these verses are tied to the previous parable of the sower and its explanation or mystery.

The passages about the secretly growing seed and the mustard seed are two parables that are specifically about the nature of the kingdom of God. For students who are interested, Morna Hooker's Bible commentary provides excellent background material.

Closing Prayer

O living and loving God, we praise you for your great gift of Jesus, your Son, whose very life is a parable, teaching us of your persistent yearning for good things for all your people and for every living thing in the universe. Help us to become parables of your Kingdom on earth. In the name of Jesus the teacher-healer we pray, Amen.

Additional Bible Helps

On the Meaning of *Kingdom of God*

Kingdom is a familiar secular word to most of us. It denotes a set of legal and political relationships between a king or queen who "rules over" his or her people. *Kingdom* implies one person in power to whom the rest owe allegiance in some way. *Kingdom* also includes the idea of having land and assets that a king or queen control and distribute. We think of European kingdoms; of African kingdoms; of Asian dynasties; of Aztec empires.

When we focus more closely on the phrase *the kingdom of God* the image gets a little hazy. Some of us may imagine a three-story universe where God as a father-king rules over a heaven that is "up there" or "out there" beyond our earthly space. Others may think of "end of the world" times when at the end of some cataclysmic event or events, Jesus will come again and God will somehow come to rule "on earth as in heaven."

People who listened to Jesus were expecting such a messiah (which means "king"). *Kingdom* meant to Jesus' listeners the hope that ultimately God's superior force would overcome the evil forces in the world.

But is this what the term *kingdom of God* meant to Jesus? Is this what it meant to the writer of Mark? Mark has Jesus begin his ministry by preaching, "The time is fulfilled, and the kingdom of God has come near; repent, and believe in the good news" (1:15). What is this king-

dom of God about which Jesus preached and taught?

Biblical scholars and theologians consider this to be a central topic of research and several different views have been presented in our century. Eduard Schweizer, in *The Good News According to Mark*, notes that in Mark 1:15 Jesus was "adopting a concept which was coined in the Old Testament [which] refers primarily to his unchallenged sovereignty in the end-time" (page 45). Further, Schweizer notes that in the Jewish religious tradition of Jesus' time, God's sovereignty meant both obeying every commandment and the time when God would reign after all the evil foes were destroyed and after all suffering was ended (page 45).

Theologian Matthew Fox, in *Original Blessing*, reviews several scholars' understandings of the phrase and notes that God's kingdom cannot be considered "a parochial or nationalistic thing; it concerns creation itself" and it concerns the "royal personhood" of us all. Thus, Fox talks of the "kingdom/queendom of God" in Mark 1:15 as having something to do with human beings in historical time (page 100-101). Quoting theologian Krister Stendahl, Fox makes a further point: "Jesus' sense of kingdom does not signify a 'rule in the heart' but a concrete effort to make right, to make just, to mend creation when it becomes broken by injustices and human violence" (page 101).

What does or will this sense of kingdom of God look like? Perhaps the writer of Mark was trying to tell his readers that the meaning and image of the term *kingdom of God* can be seen in Jesus' actions. Jesus' actions brought a little more of the Kingdom into reality each time he healed the physically, emotionally, and mentally ill and each time he included those who had been excluded by the religious "insiders." Perhaps we see a little of the kingdom of God happening each time Jesus taught that faith is really an action of persistent, consistent, and wholistic trust that God continually seeks us and wills good for us—all of us. Such an interpretation gives a new twist to that familiar prayer of Jesus "your will be done, on earth as it is in heaven." In this view the kingdom of God is both present in Jesus' actions—and ours—and yet to come as long as pain, illness, poverty, war, discrimination, and a mentality of "insiders" and "outsiders" remains present in our world.

Jesus Teaches

Several times Mark tells his readers/listeners about Jesus "teaching." However, Mark actually tells us very little of Jesus' actual teachings. A brief mention in 1:15 serves for Mark as a summary of Jesus' message. Brief sayings of Jesus are included by Mark in the "conflict stories" where Jesus is questioned or challenged by the scribes and Pharisees (see Mark 2:6-12; 2:16-17; 2:18; 2:24-28; 3:1-5). As we continue through the Book of Mark we will find that

Mark did not include an equivalent of the Sermon on the Mount. Nor did Mark share many of the parables that the other Gospel writers include. Yet Mark insisted that Jesus' teaching was a basic component of his ministry. In 4:1-9 Mark offers his readers the first in-depth teaching of Jesus—which turns out to be a parable about the parable way of teaching!

Often we think of teaching as laying out facts for students and drawing logical connections, differences, and conclusions. A parable teaches in a different way. It offers a simple story, using images and activities that will be commonly understood by the hearers. And it leaves to the hearers the job of drawing out the meaning(s).

So Jesus' first major teaching in the Book of Mark is a parable about the parable way of teaching—as well as a parable about the kingdom of God. Some would say that Mark focused on Jesus' miracles to the exclusion of his parables and major teachings. One must wonder though if Mark might not have been giving his readers (and us) a major and crucial clue: that Jesus himself is a parable for the kingdom of God. Through the word-deeds of Jesus' healings, we have a powerful image of God's ways and God's intentions for us as disciples in relation to those in need in the world. Through the word-deeds of Jesus' inter-actions with the religious leaders of his day, Jesus embodies in a wholistic way the meaning of his earlier verbal message that "the kingdom has come near."

What Is the Synoptic Problem?

The "synoptic problem" can best be observed by simply reading a passage of Mark in a book that lays out in a column format the same material in Matthew and/or Luke. Such books are called "Gospel parallels" or "synopses." In looking at a Gospel parallel, one can see immediately where the material is exact or similar in two or three of the Gospels. One also can see that some parts of each book are not to be found in the others. Synopsis of the Gospels refers to the harmony of the texts, to the generally similar view presented by Matthew, Mark, and Luke. That is why these three gospels are called "the Synoptic Gospels."

The "problem" referred to in the phrase "the synoptic problem" is really a set of research questions posed by biblical scholars: Which of these three Gospels came first? Who used whom as a reference? What other sources did they use? Did they have any other sources in common?

Some Gospel parallel books also show how some passages in the Gospel of John are "parallel to" the other Gospels. However, John is not considered one of the Synoptic Gospels because John in general is very different from the other three Gospels.

While showing how the Gospels are alike, a Gospel parallel study also shows their differences, and, in fact, some unique differences. For example, Mark shows a distinctive pattern in how he presented Jesus' disciples: they did not understand what Jesus was saying or who Jesus was. Questions about the differences and why they are different are not specifically part of the synoptic problem; rather they are literary or historical problems. Such differences only point to the value of studying the Gospels by using Gospel parallels. The synoptic problem is a question of sources.

The "solution" to "the synoptic problem" is not an absolutely established fact. Most biblical scholars hold two competing hypotheses: either Matthew or Mark was first. The "Marcan priority" is the most widely accepted solution.

Scholars who believe that Mark was written first have another problem to solve: Matthew and Luke have some material that is alike, but is not found in Mark. They explain this discrepancy by assuming that Matthew and Luke had not only Mark's manuscript to draw upon but also another source which they call *Q* (from the letter *Quelle*, the German word for *source*).

For more detail about the technical aspects of "the synoptic problem" see *Harper's Bible Commentary* (pages 943-948) or look it up in a Bible dictionary.

4

Mark
4:35—6:6a

WHO THEN IS THIS?

As we move through each session we are beginning to see more than the hero-story of a man who does "mighty works." The stories become more and more textured and richly layered with meanings. In this session, we especially focus on meanings of faith and on the human experience of being pulled from faith to fear and from fear to faith.

Opening Prayer
Magnificent God, as we continue our journey through the Book of Mark, we become more and more aware of your radical new word and action reflected in your Son Jesus. With the crowds we are amazed. With the disciples we wonder, "who then is this man that even the wind and the sea obey when he speaks?" Help us to be more in touch with our own rhythms of fear and faith. Give us courage to reach persistently toward you in an attitude of trust, even

when we are afraid. Help us to use both our hearts and our minds to come to a better understanding of you and of what it means to have faith in you. In Jesus' name we pray. Amen.

Dimension 1:
What Does the Bible Say?

(A) Map Jesus' journey.

In this session Jesus and his followers went "across to the other side" of the lake or Sea of Galilee (4:35). This "other side" is identified later on (in 5:1) as the country of the Gerasenes. Later the Gerasene demoniac proclaimed about Jesus "in the Decapolis" (5:20).
● Before trying to locate this general area on the wall map or on the map on the inside back cover of the study book, encourage students to read the entries "Gerasa" (volume 2, page 382) and "Decapolis"(volume 1, page 810) in *The Interpreter's Dictionary of the Bible*. From the Decapolis region southeast of the Sea of Galilee, Jesus again crossed over to "the other side" (5:21) back to the Galilean countryside. Finally, in the passages we will look at today (6:1), Jesus went home to Nazareth.

The inland city of Gerasa is probably not where Jesus healed the person in Mark 5:1-20. Students should be able to pick up this fact by noting in 5:2 that the man ran out of tombs (perhaps cliff side caves) to greet him as soon as Jesus "stepped out of the boat." Again, in 5:13, the swine rushed over the steep bank and drowned in the sea.

In a brief discussion note again Mark's obvious compression of the three years of Jesus' ministry. Note also Mark's lack of intention to give his readers a thorough travelogue, since so many specific details are missing! Finally, note that in this passage Jesus traveled farther afield from his hometown and home area of Galilee than he had before.

(B) Look at the woman in the crowd in three Gospels.

- Provide one or more copies of a Gospel parallel such as *Gospel Parallels: A Comparison of the Synoptic Gospels*, pages 83-85 (Thomas Nelson, 1992).
- Invite students to compare the way the three Gospel writers told the story of the woman with the flow of blood (Mark 5:25-34).
—Are there any major factual differences in the three texts? any differences in the way they were told?
—Which story seems most dramatically told?

(C) Review questions in the study book.

Invite students as they arrive to read today's passage and complete the questions if they have not already done so. Answers to Dimension 1 questions in this chapter are

1. Jairus was one of the "leaders of the synagogue" somewhere on the west side of the Sea of Galilee (some scholars say in Capernaum, but that is only a guess). He begged Jesus to come with him to his daughter who was near death. He wanted Jesus to lay his hands on her and make her well. It was unusual in Mark for one of the "establishment" religion to accept Jesus' authority or come to him for help.

2. A woman in the crowd interrupted Jesus on his way to Jairus' house. She did not intend to stop him, only to touch him. She hoped that her twelve-year menstrual flow of blood might cease and that she would be made well.

3. In these two stories, Jairus had faith that Jesus could make his daughter well. The woman in the crowd had faith that she only had to touch Jesus and she would be made well. The people from Jairus' house and the people weeping did not have faith—at least not the kind of faith that Jesus (and Mark) talked about.

Dimension 2: What Does the Bible Mean?

(D) Explore Bible meanings.

- Use the following discussion questions to explore further the two stories of Jairus and his daughter and the woman with the flow of blood. Divide the class into teams, assigning one or more questions to each team. After groups have done their research, ask them to report back to the whole class. Struggle as a whole group with meanings found. Guide them to the material in Dimension 2 in their study book, pages 31-32.
—What "case" did Mark build for his readers about the nature of faith? How was the disciples' question in Mark 4:41 pivotal to this "case"?
—What "case" did Mark build in 5:1-20 about the source of authority by which Jesus did what he did?
—How was the earlier story of Jesus' controversy with the scribes in 3:19b-35 part of Mark's "case"?
—In what ways were the beliefs and actions of Jairus like those of the woman suffering from hemorrhages?
—In what ways was the experience of the woman with the flow of blood like the experience of Jairus' daughter?
—What claims about Jesus and about faith did the evangelist Mark make in these two stories of healing?
Remember! The point is not to come to one absolute answer but rather to gain greater insight as we continue this journey through Mark. We are attempting to look anew at what Mark was trying to tell his readers about Jesus' life and message, about God's ways, and about what faith is.

(E) Do a character study.

- Invite each class member to study one of the following characters: Jairus; his daughter; people from Jairus' house; the woman with the flow of blood; Jesus' disciples in general; Peter, James, and John; the mourners at Jairus' house.
- If your class is small, one person may be assigned to each of the seven "characters." If you have fewer than seven class members, omit one or more of the following: the mourners, the people from Jairus' house, the disciples in general.
- If the class is large, several people may be assigned to each of the seven "characters."
- Ask each person or team to reread Mark 5:21-43, looking especially for (a) what their character did; (b) what their character might have been thinking; (c) how their character might have felt; (d) what faith seemed to mean to their character; (e) how their character responded to Jesus; and (f) how faith or lack of faith seemed to enter into that response.

- When the study of the characters has been finished, gather the class back together and ask them to respond to the following questions as they think their character would have responded:
—Who then is this man Jesus?
—What is he telling us?
- After every response from the class, repeat the questions to them, using their "character names":
—Jairus, who is this man Jesus and what is he telling you?
—Woman, who is this man Jesus and what is he telling you?

TEACHING TIP

Remind students to stay "in character" and to try to respond from that character's first century situation/understandings as best they can. You may need to gently repeat this guideline several times during the class' responses to the question. They, of course, cannot answer strictly out of the first century experience. The growing awareness of how we all read back into the stories from our twentieth century experience and knowledge will be helpful learning in itself. It would be good to follow this activity directly with activity (G) in order to give class members ample opportunity to share directly out of their twentieth century selves and experiences about the two healing stories.

(F) Tell the story from the woman's point of view.

- Divide the class into two teams. Assign the story of Jairus' daughter to one team and the story of the woman with the flow of blood to the other team. Give each team large newsprint sheets, a marker, and a copy of the article "A Woman's View of Women in the Bible" (see Additional Bible Helps at the end of this chapter).
- Invite each team to use all their resources and creativity to write the story from the daughter's or the woman's point of view. To get them started, suggest that they might begin each story with a paragraph where the girl says, "My name is ___ and I am twelve years old . . ." or the woman says, "My name is ___ and I . . . ." Suggest that students keep "reading between the lines" and "looking at what is not said by Mark." For example, none of the Gospel writers ever literally named the woman's problem (probably continual vaginal or menstrual bleeding which made her ritually unclean; such ritual uncleanness, which had gone on for twelve years, made her an outcast in her society; see Leviticus 15:25-30).
- When both teams have completed their stories, gather back together and have a team member read each story aloud.
- Invite reflection on what has been learned about Jesus and about faith by looking at things from a different point of view.

(G) Explore what the story characters mean to us.

- After students have responded "in character" in activity (D), invite them to come back to their twentieth century selves.
- To explore personal meanings for us today, ask the class the following questions:
—What insights have you gained from the character study activity?
—What have you learned about Jesus' message? About faith?
—What do these two interwoven stories mean to you personally?

TEACHING TIP

To encourage diversity of sharing, occasionally ask the questions: Who else has a similar insight? Who had a different insight? Do these two stories mean something different to someone else in class?

(H) Trace your journey of faith.

- On a chalkboard or sheet of newsprint draw the chart below.

Tracing My Journey of Faith

AGES	My religious experience at each age
0-7	
8-12	
13-20	
21-35	
35-50	
51-70	
71+	

AGES	What faith meant to me at each age
0-7	
8-12	
13-20	
21-35	
35-50	
51-70	
71+	

- Invite the class to open their notebook journals to a blank page. Ask them to sketch out in their notebooks or on a separate piece of paper the chart that you have drawn.
- In the first column students should write a word or draw picture symbols in each column to show what their religious experience was like at each age. Some columns might be left blank. (The following examples might help them get started: a church; a child writing in a workbook; a cross; a list of dos and don'ts; a symbol of ethical struggles; a symbol showing their denial of God or leaving the church; a symbol of prayer and meditation; a symbol of charity; a symbol of social action.)
- In the second column draw a symbol or write a phrase or sentence about what faith meant at each age. (For example, in the age 0-7 column one might draw a child's face with eyes closed and hands clasped. In the age 13-20 column, one might draw a big question mark or a symbol of commitment to Christ. Suggest to the class that in their current age box, they may want to draw a symbol or write a phrase that represents some current faith question with which they are struggling. In this way you are making it OK for them not to have a current answer to what faith is for them.)
- Discuss the following questions:
—What insights did you gain (that you want to share in the group) about your own journey as a Christian toward ever-maturing faith in God?

(I) Keep a journal on the rhythm of faith.

In your own words summarize for the class the material from the study book, Dimension 3 material on faith's flash points and on the sequence of faith and restoration. Then ask students to write in their journals. Post these steps on newsprint:
—Identify a personal experience where you wavered between fear and faith.
—What was the nature of the fear?
—What caused you to move toward an attitude of faith?
—In what ways did that faith attitude involve a basic persistent trust that God desired to restore the situation in some way?
—If you are still wavering between fear and faith, what would it mean for you to "faith" that God desires and has the ability to somehow restore this situation to wholeness?

(J) Examine a social issue.

- Ask the class: What are the major social issues in our country today that need the faithful work of God's people?
- Select one issue to examine further from the point of

view of "faithing" as a word-deed. (You may wish to review the article "Faith as a Word-Deed" presented in chapter 2, page 12 of this guide.) Do not spend a lot of time deciding on an issue! Questions to start your examination include
—What would it look like for us to have faith in relation to this issue?
—How would our attitude(s) change? (Notice the focus is on *our*, not *their*!)
—How would we name what God's desire would be for this situation? Does it look any different from "what the church teaches"? (Remember, at times Jesus reinterpreted the religious teachings of his religion!)
—If we really moved from fear to faith regarding this particular social issue, what would we be doing differently? How would we be thinking differently?

(K) Sing Scripture.

- Sing the hymn "Lonely the Boat" (The United Methodist Hymnal, No. 476).
- Compare the hymn with Mark 4:35-41 on which it is based.
—How accurately does the hymn convey the scriptural message of faith that Mark presents? (In Mark 4:35-41, Jesus had authority over the winds and waves—that is, over nature itself. For Mark this is one more piece of evidence to signal to his readers that Jesus was more than a hero or wonder-worker; Jesus was the Christ.
—How might the words be changed?
- Try writing another stanza!

Closing Prayer
O God of the winds and the waves, we yearn for your presence in our lives. So often we live in fear. So often we are caught up in the "established way" of things. So often we forget that you desire only good things for us: health and wholeness and freedom and loving relationships. Help us to catch the rhythm of this business of faithing. When we fear, help us to look anew at that fear. Help us act out our trust in your unceasing love for us. Help us to remember that it is through our faithing actions that you are able to fulfill your desire to restore us and all your peoples to wholeness. In the name of Jesus, who inspires our faith, Amen.

Additional Bible Helps

A Woman's View of Women in the Bible
Biblical scholars who are concerned to uncover or recover women's roles and experiences in biblical times have developed a number of approaches or guidelines to help them. In simplified and generalized form some of these guidelines can be stated as follows: (a) read between the

lines for what is being implied about women; (b) look for gaps in the story where the women might have been participants; (c) explore when and how the general laws and customs of that time about women were being upheld or challenged; (d) read and study with a "conscious partiality" (a phrase used by biblical scholar Elizabeth Schussler Fiorenza) rather than an attempted neutrality and objectivity; (e) be willing to open your heart and mind to a different understanding than what has been traditionally taught. Conscious partiality means knowing that we each bring to the text our own history and experience and assumptions. Men bring different experiences and assumptions than women; African-Americans bring different experiences and assumptions than Euro-Americans. However, until recent years, the only sets of assumptions and experiences we have applied to biblical materials have been white, European-oriented, and male. Now we are slowly attempting to open our hearts and our minds to other views. If we begin to apply the guidelines above, what do we learn about Jesus' relationship with women?

In light of the male-oriented culture in which he lived, Jesus' relationships with women were quite extraordinary. He treated women as fully human, equal. He never made fun of women, never blamed them for society's ills, never urged them to stay solely in the places or roles where society had confined them, never patronized them. Jesus appears to have encouraged women to become his followers, just as he encouraged men.

The intentions and attitudes of the Gospel writers, however, play an important role in how the original readers—and we today—see women in the Bible. For example, in Mark we do not hear directly about the women followers who have been with him all along until very late in the book (Mark 15:40-41) where Mark has the women standing off at a distance and appearing only when he really needed them—after the male disciples have fled. By then, of course, we have grown accustomed to reading the Gospel as a story mostly about men's interactions with Jesus. Luke, in contrast, mentions women more frequently through his Gospel, often pairing stories of women with stories of men. (See for example, Luke 2:25-38; 4:31-39; 8:1-3; 13:18-21; 15:4-10.) Scholars have speculated on why these writers' approaches were different.

Jesus taught women as well as men (as the story of Mary and Martha portrays). He also touched women as well as allowing them to touch him without censure or rebuke. Since such touching between women and men was strictly controlled by Jewish purity laws and customs in Jewish society, the story of the woman with the continuous menstrual bleeding (a fact that the male Gospel writers only indirectly refer to as "a flow of blood") is thus a profound indicator of Jesus' regard for and response to women. A menstrually bleeding woman was unclean (see Leviticus 15:19-30) and a devout Jewish man was not to touch her. Furthermore, the woman knew the laws and knew she disobeyed those laws by touching Jesus in the midst of the crowd. As a Jew, Jesus would know those same laws. Once the woman confessed her condition, those around him would likely have expected Jesus to censure her for "defiling" him. Yet he did the opposite: he affirmed her for her faith in him and he healed her of her bleeding condition.

In this case, with a little background reading on Jewish law and customs, we are able to read the Scriptures and directly obtain more understanding. At other times, with other passages, we will need to look behind the stories or look for the gaps to get an accurate picture of how Jesus viewed and treated women.

TEACHING TIP

Teachers and classes wanting to explore issues about women in the Bible or seeking additional information about studying the Bible from a woman's point of view may wish to read the following:

● *All We're Meant to Be*, by Letha Scanzoni and Nancy Hardesty (Word, 1974). See especially chapter 4, "Women in the Bible World" and chapter 5, "Woman's Best Friend: Jesus."

● *The Liberating Word: A Guide to Nonsexist Interpretation of the Bible*, by Letty M. Russell (Westminster, 1976).

5

Mark 6:6b-56

BUT THEIR HEARTS WERE HARDENED

Opening Prayer

Ever-loving, ever-seeking God, open our eyes, open our ears, open our hearts to your ever-seeking love. Help us always to trust that you are reaching out to us in love, wishing us all good things. Let our hearts not be hardened against the message that Jesus brought—and still brings through the Gospel of Mark. Help us to stay alert to your word, knowing that you speak and act in many ways. Help us to put away "old wineskins"—old traditions, old ways of seeing and speaking and knowing—that we might receive the "new wine" of the good news that Jesus taught. In his name, we pray. Amen.

Dimension 1:
What Does the Bible Say?

(A) Map Jesus' journey.

Continue tracing Jesus' ministry on the wall map—or start it now if you have not been doing it. See session 1, activity (A) for details. In today's passages, the phrase "among the villages" in Mark 6:6b could be designated by making a big loop around Galilee. (Note: Jesus was not at Herod's feast. It was probably held in Herod's palace in Tiberias.) In 6:31-32, the "deserted place" reached by boat is (by implication in 6:45) across from Bethsaida, which was a fishing village on the north end of the Sea of Galilee. In 6:46 "up on the mountain" is unknown but probably near Bethsaida somewhere. In 6:53 Gennesaret (or Ginnesar) is down the northwest coast, south of Capernaum. In 6:56 "villages or cities or farms" again probably refer to the region of Galilee.

(B) Compare "feeding the multitude" stories.

Invite students to compare the story of the feeding of the multitude in 6:30-44 with the one told later in 8:1-10. Some scholars regard this as two versions of one original event. Why might Mark have told the story twice? (Scholar Morna Hooker notes in *The Gospel According to Saint Mark* that the larger scheme in chapters 6 and 8 of Mark is parallel: a miraculous feeding followed by a journey across the lake, a discussion about bread, and a conclusion story of restoration of sight or hearing to those who lack them.) Possibly this cycle of stories was already in use in the early Christian communities before Mark wrote his Gospel.

(C) Review questions in the study book.

Invite students who have not read today's passage to do so and to write out their answers to the questions in their study books, pages 36-37.

Answers to Dimension 1 questions in this chapter:

1. One might speculate that up to the time of John's death, John was better known than Jesus.

2. Mark wanted to illustrate how the powers of the world dealt with those sent by God. Even though the method was different, John's fate anticipates Jesus' fate.

3. Like men, Mark portrays women both positively and negatively. In this case, Herodias is a willing participant in the death of John the Baptist.

4. That depends on your viewpoint! One of the outcomes to the miracle is that the disciples' understanding of their role was enlarged.

Dimension 2: What Does the Bible Mean?

(D) Add to the timeline.

Look up "Herod Antipas" (son of Herod the Great) in a Bible dictionary or in the timeline provided in chapter 1 of the study book, page 6. Add the dates of his reign (4 B.C. to A.D. 39) to the timeline (begun in chapter 1) on the wall of the classroom.

(E) Discuss the two feasts.

Use the following questions to begin your discussion of the two feasts in Mark 6. See the study book Dimension 2 material and the article in the study book "Women in the Gospel of Mark," page 40.

—Why does Mark recount at such lurid length the story of John's execution? (Could it be perhaps as a literary technique of implying time passing between sending the twelve disciples out and the time of their return? Could it be perhaps as a way to invite comparisons between John's death and Jesus' death?)

—Why did Herod have John the Baptizer beheaded?

—What is the importance of Mark's portrayal of Herodias for understanding of this Gospel's view of women?

—Which is stranger: Jesus' command that the disciples feed the five thousand or the disciples' reluctance to accept that they could?

(F) Explore variations to the story of Herod's feast.

- Review the story in 6:19-24, this time looking especially at Herodias and her daughter.
- Rewrite the story from Herodias' point of view and give it a new name.

TEACHING TIP

This activity calls for using some techniques mentioned in the article in chapter 4 (pages 21-22), "A Woman's View of Women in the Bible." The purpose here is not to rewrite the story of Jesus or his ministry, but simply to get behind Mark's point of view to see the women and their feelings, experiences, and motivations a little more clearly.

An alternate way to do this activity:

- Divide the class into two groups, one of men and one of women.
- Ask each group to write on newsprint a first person account. Instruct the men's group to write Herod's version of the story. Instruct the women's group to write Herodias' version. If your class is large, form two men's groups and two women's groups. Or have a second women's group tell Salome's version.
- When the stories have been read aloud (without comment), explore the variations.
- Ask: What insights have you gained about Mark's version of this story?

TEACHING TIP

This activity is not intended to set the men against the women, but rather to help us all to acknowledge that men and women do experience things differently. Each of us brings those experiences to the Bible as we read it. To get a more complete understanding of an event, it is important to hear more than one viewpoint.

(G) Explore the miracle stories.

- Name the miracles that Jesus performed up to the point of the story of feeding the five thousand. Urge class members to consult their Bibles.
- List the miracles on a chalkboard or newsprint.
- Group these miracle stories into two broad categories. Scholars generally group them as (1) healing stories—exorcisms and others—and (2) nature stories.

—Why does Mark tell these miracle stories?

—What was Mark trying to tell his readers about Jesus? (See the article on "Miracle Stories," page 27.)

(H) What if the invisible ones in Mark's story were made visible?

Introduce this activity with the following mini-lecture:

Mark provides rich detail for many of the events he describes. He tells us people's names, who their mothers or fathers are in some cases, and where they are from in other cases. He gives us numerical details about fishes and loaves. He includes women as primary participants in stories like the one in our last session of the woman with the flow of blood whom Jesus healed. Mark gives us details about men like Herod and John the Baptist. However, in the midst of these rich details the writer of Mark is very selective. He tells us a little about Jairus, but neglects to tell us the name of Jairus' daughter (Mark 5:22-24). He tells us the names of the brothers of Jesus but not those of his sisters (Mark 6:3). Not until the end of the whole story of Jesus does Mark tell us specifically that women were among the "followers" of Jesus. He tells us at the end—at Jesus' crucifixion—that women have been following Jesus all along and providing for him. (See Mark 16:40-41; also see scholars' discussion in *Women's Bible Commentary*, page 273.)

There are many other people whom Mark also leaves invisible. When we read Mark we have to read into the text such facts as that when Jesus interacted with crowds those crowds most likely were made up of free men, women, and children and slave men, women, and children. We have to remember that the crowds probably included rich landowners and shipbuilders, poor servants, and modest shopkeepers. The crowds probably included the very young and the very old; the able-bodied and the differently abled; the married and the unmarried. Although it is often not made clear in Mark, we know the crowds that gathered also probably included people from both the urban and the rural areas.

This "what if" activity is intended to help students discover if Mark's story looks and feels different if the invisible people are made more visible.

- Pick several verses from Mark, such as Mark 1:32-34, Mark 2:13, Mark 6:7, or Mark 6:31b. (If you have time, a good exercise in class would be to have students themselves skim through the first six chapters of Mark looking for verses where Mark has omitted details about people. Look especially for places where women, outsiders, and outcasts are left invisible.)
- Have a student read one of the selected verses aloud from a Bible. Remind each other of the context of the story.
- Reread the verse or passage, adding details in such a way as to make the invisible people more visible.

(Remember that the ones who are left invisible are often the "outcasts" or "outsiders.") Add specific details of gender, race, marital status, economic status, age, orientation, and so forth, wherever Mark has just said "they" or "the crowd" or "many" or "the Twelve" or "Jesus' disciples." (For instance, Mark 1:32-34: "That evening, at sundown, Simon and Andrew's neighbors brought their ill grandmother; a farmer who had just moved nearby from the foreign land of Egypt brought his lame son; and a prostitute brought her sick baby; . . . and all the city—rich and poor, male and female, young and old, married and unmarried, black and white, Jewish and Gentile, Egyptian and Asian, gathered around the door.")

- Reflect on the following questions:
—What did you hear?
—How did you feel?
—Did you hear the story differently? How?
—Does making the invisible people more visible in these passages do any violence to the basic message about who Jesus is and what his message is? How? Does it help? How?

Dimension 3:

Dimension 3: What Does the Bible Mean to Us?

(I) Write in journals.

- Invite students to write in their journals or on a separate piece of paper responses to questions that you have printed on chalkboard or newsprint:
—How would "feeding" and "being fed" be different for you living in this twentieth century world if you followed Jesus instead of Herod?
—How would "feeding" and "being fed" be different for you in this twentieth century Christian church if you followed Jesus instead of the "scribes and Pharisees"?

(J) Meditate on and create in art form a modern day miracle feeding.

- Invite the class to get comfortable, perhaps closing their eyes and taking several deep breaths.
- Invite students to "take in" with all their senses the story you are going to read. Then read expressively the story of the feeding of the five thousand (Mark 6:33-44). Change the words *many* and *crowd* to the words *men and women* if you wish.
- After reading the story, reflect briefly on its meaning. (Refer to the study book, page 41.)
- Offer art materials for students to create a modern day

image of a miracle-feeding event that reflects Mark's major point: God providentially nurtures all women and men and children who come, hungering, to Jesus. (See the study book, pages 40-41.) Stated another way, the point is "the expectation of God's promised redemption of all people and all things."

- Ask: If Mark were writing today in the western world, what kind of "feast image" might he use to make his point?

(K) Simulate a biblical situation in today's world.

- Assume the role of Jesus as class members assume the role of Jesus' disciples. The teacher (roleplaying Jesus) says to the disciples, "Look, the multitudes of the world have gathered here eagerly to hear God's word. They are hungry. Give them something to eat. Have a conversation among yourselves right now about how to respond to my command. Come to a decision (or a split decision if you must); then come and tell me."
- Give class members (roleplaying the disciples) time to struggle and decide; then ask for their answer to Jesus.
- Reflect on this response. The Dimension 3 study book material found on page 42 can help the class to reflect.

Closing Prayer
God, we may be unsure about many things at the end of this session. Were there important women followers of Jesus just like the twelve men? Does Jesus really expect us to go and feed all the poor of the world? What does it really mean to follow Jesus instead of Herod or the scribes? We do not all think the same way on these issues. Some of us may be a little agitated. But, God, one thing we are sure of is that you keep reaching out to us with all of your endless love. We know that even if we disagree, we are all trying to trust you and be your disciples. Keep our hearts and minds open to your fresh new living word-deed of love. In Jesus' name we pray, Amen.

Additional Bible Helps

Herodias, Herod, and John
In 6:14-29 Mark tells in much detail the story of the death of John the Baptizer. This is the only story in the Gospel of Mark where Jesus was not the focus or somehow specifically in the event described. Why did Mark devote such detail to this story? It seems artificially inserted into the narrative about Jesus and the Twelve. Perhaps Mark was trying to imply passage of time from when Jesus sent the twelve disciples out on their mission (6:7-13) to the time of their return and subsequent report to Jesus (6:30). Scholars also point to the parallels implied between John and Jesus as a reason for including the story: John and Jesus were both put to death by political leaders who knew them to be good, but who gave in to pressure from others. The story of John's death thus signals to Mark's readers the eventual death of Jesus as Mark's story continues. Mark may also have intended to draw a contrast for his readers between John and the rumors of his resurrection (6:14b, 16) and Jesus' death and resurrection.

The primary characters in this story are Herod, Herodias, and Herodias' daughter. Traditional interpretation of this story tells us that Herodias was Herod's brother's wife, whom Herod then married, and that Herodias' daughter who danced was Salome, a daughter of Philip and Herodias. Scholars now dispute several details in Mark's version of this story. Herod was not a king, but a tetrarch of Galilee and Peraea from 4 B.C. to A.D. 39. Furthermore, Mark may have been confused about Herod's family tree, which was very complex, with several persons all named Herod. Also, it appears that Philip was married to Salome, not to Herodias.

Looking beyond these errors in genealogy detail, let us look at the story of Herod's feast through the eyes of Herodias. We note that Herodias' grudge against John the Baptizer has to do with Jewish law and custom about divorce—and about the reality that men could divorce women but women could not divorce men. (See Leviticus 18:16 and 20:21.) Apparently Herodias' first husband never divorced her. Herodias was upset with John that he was questioning the legality of her marriage to Herod. Perhaps even more to the point, she was upset that John apparently had the ear of Herod and was influencing Herod's thoughts about their marriage. With no legal means at hand to protect herself or her marriage, Herodias decided to plot against John and have him killed. While we cannot condone Herodias' actions, we do need to recognize her apparent powerlessness to change her situation—or the religious community's view of her marriage—by any legal means. Sometimes centuries of traditional customs and laws that oppress some people and give other people privileges finally bring a person or a group to a point of saying: "No more!"

What about the daughter? What choices did she have? What might have happened to her if she had not obeyed her mother? Herod too seems caught in the customs and laws of his day.

Does this story begin to sound like current-day stories on the nightly TV news or in the newspapers of persons or groups whose only effective way to make their point seems to be through violence of some kind?

We may benefit from a fuller understanding of the way oppression has operated in our religious traditions. Only then will we be able to grasp a fuller heart-mind image of what Jesus meant when he said that God's kingdom had come near.

Miracle Stories

The writer of Mark tells many miracle stories as he describes Jesus' ministry in Galilee. Obviously, miracles played an important role for Mark's understanding of who Jesus was and what he was about. But what was Mark telling his readers through these miracle stories?

First, the exorcisms demonstrated that Jesus' power was great and universal: he could destroy all unclean spirits. The other healing stories (such as healing Peter's mother-in-law or the woman with menstrual bleeding) also indicated the powerful and universal nature of Jesus' power. Whenever a healing took place—even though Mark had Jesus urge secrecy, the word got out and people came from all around to be healed of their illnesses. By implication, then, Jesus had come to cleanse the world of evil forces and to restore health and wholeness to all.

Jesus' doing of miracles was tied by Mark to Jesus' teaching about the kingdom of God. The coming of the Kingdom was not just word; it was deed; it involved healings, exorcisms, restoring to health, the opening of eyes and ears of those who could not see or hear. The miracles depended on persistent, trustful yearning toward Jesus—and thus toward God. But beware! Our trustful yearnings for miracles and healings may not bring us what we think we need! God's ways of bringing wholeness and love into the world may burst our neatly organized traditions and rules and customs and beliefs! New wine requires new wineskins!

Mark used the miracle stories to reveal Jesus' identity. It was the unclean spirits who recognized Jesus' true identity when the crowds, the scribes, and even the disciples failed to recognize him. The unclean spirits called Jesus "the Holy One of God" (1:24) or "Son of the Most High God" (5:7). It is the common, often nameless women and men and children, who were cleansed of unclean spirits or healed of ailments, who by their faithful and trusting actions help portray to Mark's readers who Jesus is and what he is about. In contrast, where the people had no trust—and thus did not reach toward Jesus in actions of faith—Jesus could not do much. Mark highlighted this fact for his original readers and for us in the story of Jesus in his hometown. Jesus, amazed at the people's lack of faith, "could do no deed of power there, except that he laid his hands on a few sick people and cured them" (6:5).

Miracles—so foreign to some of us today—so basic to this story of Jesus! Can we see and hear the underlying message about faith with our hearts as well as our minds?

6

Mark 7:1-23

DO YOU NOT YET UNDERSTAND?

Opening Prayer

Mysterious God, our Creator, Redeemer, and Sustainer, we come with open hearts and open minds to hear your living Word. Like the disciples, we keep asking for explanations. We are not sure we understand what you are telling us through Jesus' words and actions. We are a little uneasy that maybe Jesus means us when he says "you hypocrites." Yet we know that we deeply yearn to keep your commandment. We want to be freed from misguided religiosity. Help us in our confusion and in our uneasiness. Truly open our hearts and minds to your ways. In the name of the Christ who continually teaches us anew, Amen.

Dimension 1:
What Does the Bible Say?

(A) Map Jesus' journey.

Continue tracing Jesus' ministry on your wall map. In Mark 7:1-23 Jesus apparently was still in the region of Galilee. In 7:24 he went to the island city of Tyre in Phoenicia on the Mediterranean coast. In verse 7:31 he went twenty-five miles up the coastline to Sidon and then crossed to the Sea of Galilee, to its southeastern edge of the Decapolis.

In 8:10 the "district of Dalmanutha" is an unknown place on the west coast of the Sea of Galilee. Some evidence in ancient manuscripts suggests that Dalmanutha and Magdala (or Magadan) may have been the same place—or two places in the same region. The Greek name for Magdala in New Testament times was Tarichea, a flourishing fishing village. In 8:13, the other side would then be the east side lake, place unknown. For more detail, look up Tyre, Sidon, and Dalmanutha in a Bible dictionary.

(B) Compare Mark and Matthew stories.

- Provide at least one Gospel parallel book for this activity. Turn to the parallel between Mark 7:1-23 and Matthew 15:1-20.
- As a class or in small groups note similarities and differences in the way Mark and Matthew tell this story of Jesus' encounter with the Pharisees. Note particularly what has been left out.

(C) Ask the scholars about the traditions of the elders.

- Provide several commentaries on Mark (for example: *The Gospel According to Saint Mark*, by Morna Hooker; *The Good News According to Mark*, by Eduard Schweizer; *Cokesbury Basic Bible Commentary*; and *Harper's Bible Commentary*), and a Bible dictionary.
- Look up Mark 7:1-5 in the commentaries. Look up "Leviticus," "Pharisees," and "Mishnah" in the Bible dictionary.
- Research the questions:
—Were the "traditions of the elders" scriptural laws?
—What was the purpose of the cleanliness customs?
- Discussion of this activity should highlight the fact that Jesus was first of all (in 7:9-13) distinguishing between the Torah (Jewish Scripture) and the "traditions of the elders," which were the traditions that the Pharisees had built up over the centuries. Then Jesus went on to a more radical answer that challenged even the Torah for its "demands for Levitical purity" (*The Gospel According to Saint Mark*, page 173).

(D) Review the questions in the study book.

- If students are not completing these questions before class, offer time at the beginning of class. Answers to the study questions are as follows:

1. The "tradition of the elders" that Jesus' disciples were violating was eating with defiled hands, that is without washing. The purpose of this custom was not hygiene but seems to have originated with priests who ceremonially washed before eating "holy" food that had been used in a sacrifice. (See the study book, page 45 in Dimension 2.)

2. Human tradition was always less important to Jesus than the commandment of God. In this case, verses 6-7 shed light on the situation. The religious leaders were intent on keeping rituals described in the law; Jesus understood the law to be intent on human compassion.

3. This is a subjective question. It would seem, however, that thoughts, desires and motivations produce actions rather than the reverse.

Dimension 2: What Does the Bible Mean?

(E) Discuss Jesus' meaning and Mark's intentions.

Discuss the following questions:
—What was the difference, for Jesus, between "the commandment of God" and "human tradition" (Mark 7:8-9)? See the study book, page 47. The distinction between the human tradition of extending a biblical precept (ritual cleanliness of the priests) into a nonbiblical tradition (ritual handwashing of all Jews before eating) is clarified. The larger issue here, which Mark touches on lightly and awkwardly, is Jesus' concern with 'hollow worship,' which lacks true connection with and reverence for God and God's commandment to "love your neighbor as yourself."
—What was the significance of Mark's parenthetical statement in 7:19b that Jesus thus declared all food clean?
—Why is it important to Mark's readers? Remember that Mark's readers are likely Gentile rather than Jewish. Mark's Gospel is reflecting the growth of Christianity beyond its Jewish roots. Early Christians were having to determine whether obeying all the Jewish laws and rituals was necessary for one to be Christian. We are more familiar with this great debate through Paul and the issue of circumcision. Other similar debates down through history include whether or not women can be ordained; whether or not heterosexuals are the only ones who can be fully Christian; how to treat persons of different racial backgrounds.
—What is the significance of Mark's recalling the feeding of the multitudes at this point in his Gospel story of Jesus?

This passage seems to be more of Mark's writing technique of underscoring the disciples' lack of understanding of the true meaning of God's kingdom. The references to the feeding of the multitudes would seem to imply that with God there is always more than enough, that the power-grace-love of the Kingdom overflows.

(F) Stage a "gentle" debate on an issue facing the early Christian church.

- Divide the class into two teams: (a) the Pharisees and scribes, and (b) the followers of Jesus.
- Have each team choose a spokesperson. (The rest of the team will sit behind/beside that person to "coach.")
- Pose this question for debate: Do you agree that only that which comes out of a person can defile, and nothing that goes in can defile (Mark 7:15)? Why or why not?

- The "Followers Team" should present the "yes" argument, while the "Pharisee Team" presents the "no" argument.
- Give the teams time to formulate responses within their team. (They may want to consult commentaries or Bible dictionaries on Jewish ritual purity in Leviticus and on scholars' interpretations of Jesus' remarks.)
- Spokespersons should make their opening statements. Further responses from each side can be "coached" by team members.

- After the debate discuss the question: What is the meaning of the Isaiah passage that Jesus used in Mark 7:8: "You abandon the commandment of God and hold to human tradition"?
- Follow up this activity with activity (G).

Dimension 3:
What Does the Bible Mean to Us?

(G) Stage a "gentle" debate on a modern issue.

- Assign the "Pharisee Team" from activity (F) to become the "Radical Jesus Followers of the 1990's" and the "Followers Team" from activity (F) to become the "Pillars of the Church of the Twentieth Century." Pose one of these questions for debate:
—Should the church change its traditional understanding that the disciples were all male? Why or why not?
—Should the church change its traditional understanding that *family* means a married couple with children? Why or why not?
—Should the church change its traditional understanding that self-avowed practicing homosexual persons should not be ordained? Why or why not?
- Give teams time to formulate their arguments and "coach" their spokespersons.
- After the debate, discuss the question: What is the meaning of the Isaiah passage that Jesus used in Mark 7:8: "You abandon the commandment of God and hold to human tradition"?

(H) Write in journals.

- Write these questions on a chalkboard or sheet of

newsprint as suggestions for focusing students' journal writing:
—What is the commandment of God?
—What does it mean to honor that commandment?
—How is that commandment different from human traditions?
—How might we as a church be rejecting the commandment of God in order to keep our traditions?

(I) Discuss meanings about religious tradition and discipleship.

Use questions from Dimension 3 material in the study book, page 50, for group discussion:
—What is it in your religious tradition that means practically everything to you? To what are you absolutely committed? What is Jesus' response?
—What is it, in your understanding and practice of being Christian, that obviously and indispensably sets you apart from those who are not Christian? What is Jesus' response?
—What boundaries, traditions, or standards of religiosity are we (personally, as a local church, or as a denomination) setting and then expecting God to applaud and approve? What is Jesus' response?
—How does "having faith" differ from scriptural laws, religious customs, and Christian morality? What is Jesus' response?

(J) Sing a spiritual.

Invite the class to sing the African-American spiritual "Lord, I Want to Be a Christian," which is mentioned in Dimension 3 of the study book. (The word *God* might be an interesting substitution for the word *Lord*.) See the sidebar for other words to sing to the music. Create other stanzas that expand the song's understanding of what it means to be a Christian.

Lord [God], I Want to Be a Christian

Stanza 1:
Lord [God], I want to be more loving in my heart.
Stanza 2:
Lord [God], I want to be inclusive of your folk.
Stanza 3:
Lord [God], I want to feed the hungry on your streets.
Stanza 4:
Lord [God], I want to touch the lonely with your love.
Stanza 5:
Lord [God], I want to be like Jesus every day.

(K) Sculpt an image of being a Christian.

- Pause in your singing of the spiritual in activity (J) to invite persons to use clay to create their image or sculpture of the idea of being a Christian. Class members may want to work together to create a group sculpture.
- Quietly sing or hum the spiritual while people work with the clay. When people have finished, invite persons to show their image and to say something about its meaning for them.

TEACHING TIP

You will need to purchase modeling clay or dough or prepare a recipe of homemade dough. See the sidebar. Adults may be hesitant to work with clay, thinking it either "child's play" or something only an artist does. Encourage them to experiment with the feel of the clay, then how shapes and forms can be made and remade. Encourage participants to focus on the singing or humming of the spiritual and let their hands move with the music. Even if adults do not end up with a definite sculpture, they may likely have had a significant experience about the meaning of being Christian.

Modeling Compound

This recipe is sufficient for at least two adults to use for the activity.

- 2 cups flour
- 1 cup salt
- 2 tablespoons salad oil
- water to mix
- oil of wintergreen (optional)

Mix the first three ingredients together in a bowl.

Slowly add water to the mixture until the dough is pliable. Knead the mixture well.

Add oil of wintergreen to the dough to help prevent it from spoiling.

Store the dough in an airtight container until ready to use.

(L) Discuss other passages from weekly readings.

- Read aloud Mark 7:24-30.
  Note that in Mark 7:24-30 Jesus treated the Gentile woman differently from the earlier Jewish men and women whom he healed. With them Jesus immediately responded with healing and praised them for their faith. Some scholars see this as a clue to the beginning of Jesus' Gentile mission; other scholars disagree. It is significant, however, that Mark has placed this story right after the story about Levitical distinctions of clean and unclean. The way Jesus acted seems out of character, but it is unlikely that the story was invented. Jesus himself probably confined his ministry to Jews, which is understandable given the Jewish emphasis on Israel as God's elect. Jesus' healing miracles were closely connected in Mark to his preaching of the coming of God's kingdom: Israel was to repent and believe. The woman's answer was an acceptance of that emphasis, and Jesus responded positively to her understanding. Again, as Mark has noted over and over, it was one outside of Israel's establishment who understood Jesus.
- Read aloud Mark 8:14-15.
  In Mark 8:14-15 Jesus referred to "the yeast of the Pharisees," which the NRSV New Oxford Annotated Bible explains as hypocrisy that spreads the Pharisees' influence by means of their teachings, and "the yeast of Herod," which is worldliness and irreligion.

Closing Prayer

God of the past, the present, and the future, we are somewhat puzzled by Mark's stories today. We also feel somewhat threatened, for Jesus seems to be challenging some of our long-held beliefs and religious traditions. It is hard to let go of familiar ways of listening to your word, God. We are uncomfortable when we hear Jesus' harsh words to the Pharisees and think that maybe Jesus is speaking to us too. Have we—like the Pharisees and scribes—hung onto certain beliefs and traditions so much that we have rejected your own commandment? Help us to be clear about what it means to "be a Christian." In the name of the Christ who came to free us, Amen.

Additional Bible Helps

Faith and Religious Observance

"Is faith the same as religious observance? Can the commitment of religious people, devotion even of the highest sort and driven by the loftiest of intentions, obstruct the purposes of God?" These are the questions that open chapter six of the study book—and these are the questions put to us at the end of chapter six.

The answers from Jesus in Mark are "no" and "maybe." Both answers verge on meddling with some of our most precious beliefs. Perhaps we, like the Pharisees and the disciples, "just don't get it!" We continue to want to look at our Christian faith as a set of rules to live up to and religious observances to perform according to long established tradition. Jesus said, "No, faith is not observing religious customs or obeying religious laws; faith is absolute trust in God's abundant grace and love for all of God's people. Faith is trust in God's ability to feed, to heal, to bring back to life what was dead."

Then comes the "maybe" part. Maybe our customs of worship, our traditional religious rules, our traditional sense of what is morally right or wrong—maybe those things will help us in the faith-trust business. Perhaps they will not. Perhaps they help some, but cause others to stumble. Or maybe they help us, but also serve to keep others "outsiders." Perhaps a traditional religious law or custom is a true help to all of God's people, helping all people to engage in faith as trust in God.

The trick is knowing which ones—and what to do with our long-held beliefs and customs if they turn out to be obstructing our own or someone else's faith as trust in God.

Such struggles are happening in major ways at the national levels of various denominations (around issues of women's participation and leadership, ethnic participation and leadership, children and youth participation and leadership and gay/lesbian participation and leadership). But such struggles may also be manifesting themselves in other kinds of struggles in our local churches. Are we holding on to traditional ways of worship, traditional use of male language, traditional assumptions about who can be trustees, or on the pastor-parish committee, or lay leaders? Are we crying about the loss of members while refusing to reach out to those unchurched ones around us because they are "different" in some way and thus, in our minds perhaps "sinful" or "not eligible" to be Christians with us?

What would Jesus say to us today? Would he confront us as modern-day Pharisees? Would he praise us for our faith? Ouch!

7

Mark 8:22—9:1

How Then Is It Written About the Son of Man?

Opening Prayer

Dear God, we want to be like Jesus. We want to be more loving, more holy, more faithful. We think we know what that means and we try our best. Yet often we get caught up in the rhythms of our long-held beliefs and long-practiced customs. Sometimes we have lost track of their original source or purpose. Open our eyes to the radical new word-deed that you offer in Jesus. Help us to practice our faith as we look once again at who Jesus really is and what he calls us to do and be. Amen.

Dimension 1: What Does the Bible Say?

(A) Map Jesus' journey.

- Continue tracing Jesus' journey on the wall map.
- Use Bibles and look up each place in a Bible dictionary. Jesus' movements include the following:

Mark 8:22—Bethsaida at the north end of the Sea of Galilee

Mark 8:27—Caesarea Philippi, an ancient Gentile city-state on the southern slope of Mount Hermon in northern Palestine

Mark 9:2—an unknown mountain where the Transfiguration event took place (although tradition says it was Mount Tabor, which is six miles east/southeast of Nazareth)

Mark 9:33—north to Capernaum on the Sea of Galilee.

(B) Compare Peter's confession in the Gospels.

- Read the information found in the article, "On Peter's Confession and Jesus' Response," in the Additional Bible Helps section at the end of this session. Share this information with the class.
- Divide into small groups and provide a Gospel parallel, commentaries, and Bible dictionaries for each group or plan for the groups to share these resources.
- Ask groups to look up Mark 8:27-33 in a Gospel parallel and compare Peter's and Jesus' conversation in Mark with the conversation recorded in Matthew and Luke (Matthew 16:13-28 and Luke 9:18-27).

- Read in commentaries to gain a better insight about what scholars think about the differences in the telling of this story in these three Gospel accounts.
- Read about "Messiah," "Jewish Messiah," and "Christ" in Bible dictionaries.
- Ask groups to prepare a brief report to be presented later during class.

(C) Review questions in the study book.

- Again, provide time for students at the beginning of class to complete the questions.

Answers to questions in the study book follow:

1. The general public saw Jesus as a prophet like John the Baptist or Elijah, who was thought by some to be the one who would come and rescue Israel.

2. Peter, with sudden great insight (according to the way Mark tells it), spoke for the other disciples and said Jesus was the Messiah (or "the Christ").

3. Jesus responded to Peter by sternly ordering Peter and the other disciples "not to tell anyone about him."

(D) What is the Passion prediction?

- Locate the first and second "passion predictions" (Mark 8:31 and 9:30-31).
- Research the word *passion* in a Bible dictionary.
- Answer the question: What is "the passion of Jesus?"

Dimension 2:
What Does the Bible Mean?

(E) Look at the heart of Mark's Gospel.

- Pose the following questions for research. Use the study book and commentaries to find answers.
- The study book says Mark 8:27—9:1 is "the heart of Mark's Gospel." What is contained in that passage? Why is it considered "the heart"?
- Why does Mark introduce the conversation at Caesarea Philippi (8:27-33) with the story of the blind man's healing at Bethsaida (8:22-26)?
- How is the story of the blind man at Bethsaida connected to the healing of the deaf man in 7:31-37? How is the story related to the blindness of the disciples in 8:13-21? What is Mark's point?

(F) Dramatize Peter's confession.

- Prepare six copies of the following dramatized version of Mark 8:27-30 and recruit students to read it dramatically while "walking along."

- After the skit, use the following questions for general discussion.

> NARRATOR: Jesus and his followers left for the villages of Caesarea Philippi. While they were walking along, he questioned them.
>
> JESUS: Who do people say I am?
>
> DISCIPLE 1: Some say you are John the Baptizer come back to life.
>
> DISCIPLE 2: Others say you are Elijah.
>
> DISCIPLE 3: Others say you are one of the prophets.
>
> JESUS: But you—who do you say I am?
>
> PETER: You are the Christ.
>
> NARRATOR: And Jesus gave them strict instructions.
>
> JESUS: Say nothing to anyone about me.
>
> *Copyright 1994 by Cokesbury.*
> *Permission granted to photocopy this sidebar.*

- —What is the religious significance of the various answers as to how Jesus was regarded by the general public of his time? (See study book, Dimension 2, page 54.)
- —Why did Jesus sternly order his disciples not to tell anyone about him? (Mark 8:30) Explore the idea of the "messianic secret." (See the sidebar in the study book on page 55, "The Theme of Secrecy.")
- —What might Peter have said to Jesus after hearing Jesus talk about his coming suffering, death, and Resurrection? (Check Matthew 16:22 for Matthew's version.)

TEACHING TIP
If students did activity (B), ask them to report on how Matthew and Luke tell this story differently and how scholars account for the differences. If students did not do activity (B), use material from "On Peter's Confession and Jesus' Response" found in the Additional Bible Helps section in an informal "mini-lecture." Follow up this activity with the journaling activity (L) in Dimension 3.

(G) What is a Gospel?

- Present a mini-lecture to students using the information from the article "What Is a Gospel?" found in the Additional Bible Helps at the end of this session. An alternative way to present this information would be to enlist a student ahead of time to study the material and present it to the class.
- This activity is intended as preparation for activity (J) in Dimension 3 where students will begin to create a modern "gospel."

(H) Sing Scripture as you explore the Transfiguration.

- Provide copies of hymnals to the group. Locate hymns that are based on the Mark passage about the transfiguration of Jesus. Two possibilities found in the *The United Methodist Hymnal* are
- —"O Wondrous Sight! O Vision Fair" (No. 258)
- —"Christ, upon the Mountain Peak" (No. 260)
- Sing the hymns, then compare the words of the hymn with the Scripture.
- —Does the hymn portray the sense of the Scripture accurately?
- —How would you change the hymn words to convey the scriptural idea better today? Does it need another verse? Can you create it?

Dimension 3:
What Does the Bible Mean to Us?

(I) Lead a guided meditation on being a Christian.

- Invite students to get comfortable, close their eyes if they wish, and breath slowly and deeply several times. Sing softly together one verse of "Lord, I Want to Be a Christian." Read expressively all or part of the background article, "On the Meaning of Being a Christian," found at the end of this session in the Additional Bible Helps section.
- Then sing the words "God, I want to be like Jesus" to the same tune.
- Move directly from this activity into the journaling activity.

(J) Write a modern version of a gospel.

- Provide newsprint and markers or other paper and pencils.
- Ask students to imagine that they are disciples of the Christ in the late twentieth century. Their assignment is to write a gospel to their contemporaries who are not Christian. They must tell the story of Jesus. Suggest that they consider the following questions as they work on writing their gospel.
- —What will you tell them? How will you open your gospel?
- —What events will you highlight or omit?
- —How will you portray Jesus' followers? disciples?
- —How do you get across the message of Jesus as the Christ and the message of what faith is?
- Have students write a first gospel chapter.

(K) Write in journals.

- Pose one or more of these questions to students for their personal writing and reflection. Write the questions on chalkboard or newsprint so that students can refer back to and reflect on them as often as they need to while writing.
- —Who do YOU say that Jesus is?
- —What are you looking for in a messiah?
- —What is the meaning of Jesus' death on the cross for you personally?

(L) What's different? What's the same? Why?

- Ask the class: What is different now that the Messiah has come—in the world? in people's spiritual lives? in the church? List answers in a column on chalkboard or newsprint.
- Then ask: What is the same even though the Messiah has come? List answers in a second column.
- Finally, ask:
- —Why are things different? the same?
- —Is this a reflection of faith and discipleship or a lack of faith and discipleship?
- —How?

(M) Create a litany prayer with a hymn response.

- Provide newsprint, markers, and copies of *The United Methodist Hymnal* for the group. Turn to the hymn, "Heal us, Emmanuel, Hear Our Prayer" (No. 266). This hymn is based on Mark 9:14-27.
- Reread Mark 5:25-34 and Mark 9:14-27. Then create prayer lines to be alternated between the verses of the hymn.
- At the end of this session pray the litany prayer, singing the hymn response.

(N) Prepare an assignment for next week.

- Interview someone whom you consider to be a disciple of Jesus. Find out how they view discipleship.

- Bring newspaper or magazine clippings of persons and events that represent "discipleship" to you.

Closing Prayer

Eternal, ever-loving, creating God, we are still struggling to hear your living Word for us today. Some of us are confused about the predictions of Jesus' death and what they mean. We're still not sure how to truly answer the question "who is this man Jesus?" But we deeply yearn to have our ears and eyes opened to the fullness of your message. Help us as we continue on our journey with the Gospel of Mark. Give us greater insight into the true meanings of discipleship. Amen.

Additional Bible Helps

On Peter's Confession and Jesus' Response

We have seen over and over in Mark that the disciples "just didn't get it" as far as understanding who Jesus really was. Then, suddenly at Caesarea Philippi (an ancient city-state that was largely pagan), Peter gained a sudden insight: Jesus was the Christ, the Messiah. But, what did Peter mean by the use of the term *Messiah*? Perhaps Jesus' rejection in Mark was because the disciples had not yet understood Jesus as the suffering "Son of Man." Perhaps their understanding of *messiah* was that of the righteous divine king who would restore Israel and reign over it in idyllic times. Whatever the reason, Mark remained true to his technique and theme of secrecy about Jesus' identity. Jesus commanded the disciples not to talk about their new understanding of him—and he turned to teaching them about the coming suffering that the Son of man would endure.

In contrast, in Matthew the disciples are portrayed all along in a more positive light; by this time in Matthew they were well on their way to understanding who Jesus was (See *Harper's Bible Commentary*, page 968, for more background.) Perhaps also Matthew may have felt his readers needed direct affirmation that Peter spoke the truth; whereas Mark felt his readers would surely know it by this point in the book, even if the disciples' eyes were not really opened until after Jesus was put to death.

Luke's version of this story is very brief and lacks the stern response of Jesus to Peter that is found in Mark. Some scholars point to this omission as evidence that Luke was holding Peter in higher regard, but the whole story seems to be told with less clarity in details and, typical of Luke, is wrapped in prayer, a Lukan technique to alert readers to the importance of a passage. (See *Harper's Bible Commentary*, page 1027, for more detail.)

On the Meaning of Being Christian

"Lord, I want to be a Christian . . . ." What does it mean "to be a Christian"? Mark's Gospel tells a story of a wandering miracle worker who was more than that. Mark's story is of a Jesus whose words and deeds were one: Jesus preached that the "kingdom of God has come near"; Jesus healed persons because of their total faith in his (and God's) ability to do so, thus visibly demonstrating that the Kingdom was near.

Mark leads us onward in the Gospel story to a Jesus who upset the established leaders of the Jewish religion of his times. Why? Because he did not just pass on to the common folk what the Pharisees had taught; he reinterpreted and sometimes flatly rejected their teachings. Jesus was an insider preaching to insiders who did not understand his message of the Kingdom and who thus turned him into an outsider—someone dangerous to the traditional faith of Israel.

Who did hear Jesus' message loud and clear? The outsiders: the persons possessed of demons and unclean spirits, the woman with the continual bleeding that made her ritually unclean and an outcast in Jewish life, the deaf and the blind ones, and even the Gentile woman whose daughter was possessed of an unclean spirit. Jairus, as a leader of the synagogue, was an exception to Mark's litany of the ones who had faith—that element of complete trust in and dependence on God that Jesus also lifted up in his comments about children.

The people who saw and heard Jesus in action responded with amazement at his "new teaching" (1:27), and they raised questions about why he and his disciples did not follow established Jewish traditions (2:18). But the scribes and Pharisees responded to Jesus' early words and deeds with harsh judgment (2:6-7) and gathered to plot against him (3:6). Jesus' interactions with the Jewish religious establishment were confrontational. He reinterpreted their traditions and even the Torah (the law) by declaring all foods to be clean. He warned the crowd to beware of the 'yeast of the Pharisees' who perpetuate hollow forms of worship.

Who was this man who caused such wide variation of response? Was he a young upstart challenging his religious elders and misusing Scripture? a miracle worker? a charlatan possessed by Satan? a revolutionary bent on making himself "king of the Jews"? a resurrected John the Baptizer warning of the end of history? a new Moses bringing new Law? a perfectly righteous messiah-king who would rule over Israel in an idyllic future? the suffering Son of God and Son of man? the one who healed the afflicted, welcomed the outcasts, ate with sinners, and upset the religious leaders and their traditions?

"God, I want to be like Jesus. . . ." But who was this man—and what does it mean to follow him? How can I "be like Jesus"?

What Is a Gospel?

The word *gospel* is derived from the Anglo-Saxon word *godspell*, which means "good tidings" or "good news." As far as we know, the writer of the Gospel of Mark was the first to create a gospel. A gospel tells the "good tidings" of Jesus the Christ. Again, as far as we know, Jesus left no written materials about his own thoughts, words, or deeds. What we know of Jesus originally came from the oral sayings and stories that Jesus' original followers told to others after his death. Mark had these oral sayings and stories and most probably a written source, which had been collected together for the early Christian church. From these sources Mark created the first Gospel—a whole new literary form.

Scholars mostly believe that the Gospel was written to be shared orally with early Christians. It was probably read as a whole or perhaps in large sections. Some scholars speculate that Mark was a theater-goer who utilized theatrical techniques to create his "good tidings" about Jesus the Christ. For example, the opening of Mark is often compared to the prologue of a Greek play, sung by a chorus to introduce the theme. Also, the repetition of words, phrases, and stories would have been helpful to listeners.

Though we traditionally have seen the Gospel of Mark divided into chapters and verses, the original probably was not in such a form. Mark probably made use of oral and written collections of miracle stories, parables, and sayings of Jesus. If in fact the writer was also a disciple of Peter, he would have heard Peter telling his stories of Jesus. Mark wove these materials together and added transitional material to help him tell the story of Jesus more fully. In addition, the writer of Mark left us with a distinct new literary form by the way he organized and presented his material.

8

Mark 10:1-52

To Enter the Kingdom of God

LEARNING MENU

Keep in mind your students, their needs and interests, and how they seem to learn best. Choose at least one activity from Dimensions 1, 2, and 3. If you are offering small group activities as students arrive, activities (A), (C), (H) and (I) are good possibilities.

Opening Prayer

Ever gracious and loving God, we confess that sometimes we portray the idea that being a disciple of Jesus is easier than it really is, forgetting what it really requires of us. We settle for rules to follow, as if we can earn our way into the Kingdom. We fuss over who is greatest, as if the greatest ones were going to get into the Kingdom. We look for magic formulas of salvation, as if those formulas of salvation will get us into the Kingdom. Like Jesus' disciples we keep missing the point, so Jesus tells us more stories. Open our hearts and our minds to the simplicity—and the demand—of being a disciple. In Jesus' name we pray, Amen.

Dimension 1: What Does the Bible Say?

(A) Continue to map Jesus' journey.

● Continue to track the journeys of Jesus on the class map. Use the following information to do so:

—Mark 10:1. From Capernaum Jesus and his followers went south through Samaria and "beyond the Jordan," which is a phrase that translates an Aramaic or Hebrew form of the name Perea. Perea is bounded on the west by the Jordan River and the northeast shore of the Dead Sea; on the east by the districts of Gerasa, Philadelphia, and Hesbon; on the north by the city of Pella; and on the south by the Herodian fortress of Machaerus, where John the Baptist was executed. They probably crossed the Jordan on a Roman road northeast of Bethel.

—Mark 10:32. "On the road, going *up* to Jerusalem" probably refers to the fact that Jerusalem is 2,500 feet above sea level and the Jordan River is below sea level.

—Mark 10:46. They came to Jericho and then left it while still on their way to Jerusalem.

(B) View a video of southern Palestine.

- View the part of the video in the *Bible Teacher Kit* on southern Palestine, watching particularly for the areas where Jesus traveled on his journey south into Jerusalem.

(C) Compare stories of the rich man.

- Use copies of the Gospel parallels and commentaries on Matthew, Mark, and Luke to examine three stories of the rich man: Mark 10:17-31; Matthew 19:16-30; and Luke 18:18-30. (*Harper's Bible Commentary* provides a concise, helpful summary of these stories.)
- Have students ask themselves the following questions:
—How are the stories alike?
—How are they different?
—What do commentators say about the meanings of the story?

(D) Review questions in the study book.

- Provide time for arriving students to write answers to the questions in Dimension 1 if they have not done so. Briefly review the answers, especially if you are not choosing activity (E).
- Answers to these questions are as follows:
  1. The Pharisees asked Jesus, "Is it lawful to divorce?" Jesus responded initially by asking them what Moses said about divorce. Hearing the Pharisees' response, Jesus said that God's intention was for marriage. Divorce was permitted because humans had not lived up to God's intention.
  2. Children are welcome in the kingdom of God. Adults need to be like children as they receive the Kingdom.
  3. Jesus tells the man who wants to inherit eternal life to give his wealth away to the poor. The event illustrates the cost of discipleship.
  4. He merely says that it is extremely difficult. One cannot have a higher priority than the kingdom of God and expect to enter the Kingdom. Only by relying upon God can one enter the Kingdom.
  5. These stories pertain to the setting of proper priorities for disciples.

(E) Capture the big picture of Mark.

- Use the article "Looking at the Passion Narratives" in Additional Bible Helps at the end of this session as a mini-lecture to review the material in the study book on the repetitive structure of Mark. Do this activity before moving into Dimension 2 activities.

Dimension 2: What Does the Bible Mean?

(F) Ask the scholars about children and the rich.

- Divide the class into four teams. Give each team one of the following questions. Ask them to research possible answers to these questions. Offer commentaries and remind them to review material from Dimension 2 of the study book, pages 63-64. Provide time for teams to report their findings.
—What does it mean to receive the kingdom of God as a little child? What does it not mean? (Mark 10:13-16)
—Is Jesus saying that poverty is intrinsically better than wealth, that the poor are more blessed than the rich? (Mark 10:17-22)
—Why were the children able to receive Jesus' blessing (Mark 10:16) when the rich man could not (Mark 10:22)?
—How does the saying in Mark 10:31 sum up Jesus' teaching about children, wealth, and self-renunciation?

(G) Prepare a dramatic reading on wealth and status.

- Assign students the parts of the RICH MAN, JESUS, several DISCIPLES (10:26), and PETER with the teacher serving as a NARRATOR.

- Invite the rest of the class to pick one of the following characters they will listen to closely and try to identify with the rich man, the disciples, or Peter.
- Read the story (Mark 10:17-31) as dramatically as possible. Add dramatic movement if you wish.
- Discuss the following questions:
—What did you hear?
—What did you feel?
—How are we like the rich man?
—How are we like the disciples?
—How are we like Peter?
—What does Jesus mean by "many who are first will be last, and the last will be first"?

Dimension 3: What Does the Bible Mean to Us?

(H) Continue writing a modern gospel.

- Focus in this session on which parables and healing stories you want to tell—or how else you might convey to contemporary non-Christians Jesus' message of the Kingdom and the meaning of faith.
- Provide newsprint and markers.

(I) Create a montage of clippings on discipleship.

- Provide newspapers and magazines for students to use in searching for stories and pictures of persons and events that represent acts of discipleship. Inform students that they will use this material to create a montage.
- In the center of a large posterboard, print "Modern Discipleship." Arrange the clippings around the heading. While working, share the stories of the clippings informally.

TEACHING TIP
Montage means a collection of similar items that are arranged into a pleasing composite picture. Some clippings may be arranged at angles; others may overlap each other for artistic effect.

(J) What do you think about discipleship?

- Hang two sheets of newsprint on a wall with the following headings:
—"Discipleship is. . ."
—"Discipleship is not. . ."
- Invite students to write their responses. At some point in the session look at and discuss their responses.

(K) Share interviews.

- Provide time for students to tell about their interviews if you made this assignment last week.
- After hearing these stories, explore the question: What makes these people good examples of someone you consider to be a disciple of Jesus?

TEACHING TIP
If your class is large, divide it into several groups, or have pairs share stories so as not to take up too much class time.

(L) Continue to write in personal journals.

- Write on chalkboard or newsprint the following questions:
—What hinders me from becoming a follower of Jesus?
—What would I do differently if I truly lived life now as a pure gift from God (like a child)?

TEACHING TIP
See the study book, pages 66-67, for help with journal questions.

(M) Consider the phrase "sitting loosely with our possessions."

- Read together Mark 10:46-52.
- Discuss the following questions:
—How did blind Bartimaeus treat his possession (his cloak)?
—What would it mean for us to "sit loosely enough with what we possess" that we might enter the kingdom of God as Bartimaeus did? (See the study book, page 65).
—How might our ways of worship or our rules about moral behavior be like possessions or stumbling blocks that keep us from entering the kingdom of God?

(N) Write a script on discipleship.

- Create a script (based on Mark 10:35-40) to accompany the hymn "Are Ye Able" (No. 530, *The United Methodist Hymnal*). The script should lift up modern-day images to illustrate the verses of the hymn.
- Consider the following questions:
—What does it mean to be crucified to the death?
—Does it mean only physical death?
—How are losses of friends, family, financial security, career, and so forth also crucifixions?
—Who is the modern thief and what does it mean that the thief is worthy?
—How are we thieves in this context?

—Does the third stanza of this hymn mean only physical death?

—What other deaths do we die as disciples?

—Who are the "heroic spirits" (mentioned in the fourth stanza) of our age?

—When are we the "heroic spirits"?

Closing Prayer

Ever-loving God, friend of the poor, the powerless and the outcast—all those who are last in our eyes and first in yours, we too are ever seeking to enter into your divine realm. Help us to sit loosely with our possessions that we might cast them off if need be in order to enter your Kingdom. Help us to sit loosely with our religious customs and traditions that we might revise them if need be in order to enter your Kingdom. Give us courage to live as one who is last and least in this world as we seek to be disciples of Jesus.

Additional Bible Helps

Looking at the Passion Narratives

The writer of the Gospel of Mark was creating something new—a form of written material that had never existed before. We have been studying Mark's stories about Jesus and Jesus' basic messages in those stories and healing actions. Look at how Mark wove all these stories of Jesus together.

Mark used two major "outlines" or "frameworks" of ideas as a base for his Gospel. One was a geographical outline. The other was a theological framework.

Look at the geographical framework of the Gospel first. Mark began his good tidings with Jesus' **baptism at the Jordon River**; moved to his **ministry in Galilee**; then his **ministry beyond Galilee** (to Tyre and Sidon, the Decapolis, and finally Caesarea Philippi); then his **journey down the Jordon toward Jerusalem**. The story climaxed geographically at the end of the book—with Jesus' **death in Jerusalem and the empty tomb**.

Look at the theological framework that Mark appears to have used. The commentator on Mark in *Harper's Bible Commentary* calls Mark's theological framework "architectonic," which simply means that the climax or focus theologically comes in the middle of the book rather than at the end. As the commentator says "The units are structured like an arch where events on the side panels . . . draw the onlooker to gaze to the main themes in the center" (page 984).

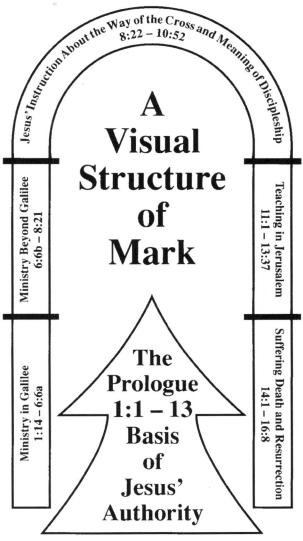

Adapted from description in *Harper's Bible Commentary*, page 984.

The left side of the arch is made up of Part I (**Jesus' ministry in Galilee**—Mark 1:14-6:6a) and Part II (**Jesus' ministry beyond Galilee**—Mark 6:6b–8:21). The right side of the arch is made up of Parts IV (**teaching in Jerusalem**—Mark 11:1–13:37) and Part V (**the suffering, death, and Resurrection**—Mark 14:1–16:8) Both sides point toward the center of the arch, which is Part III (**instruction about the way of the cross and the mean-**

ing of discipleship—Mark 8:22–10:52). While the commentator does not divide out the prologue, we will do it here. The prologue serves as a kind of "road sign" or "welcome mat"—telling us what and who is ahead!

We must remember that the writer of Mark created the written manuscript to be read orally, probably as a whole, or at least in very large "chunks" to the early Christian community with which he was affiliated. Thus Mark did not give us these divisions of the book. In fact any divisions at all are probably those of later scribes, scholars, and interpreters.

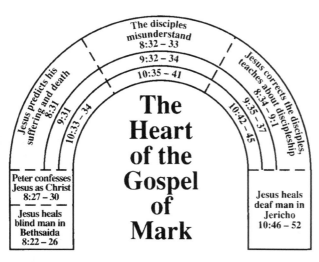

Adapted from description in *Harper's Bible Commentary*, page 984.

However, with this structure in mind to help us, look at the centerpiece of Mark's Gospel (the tip of the arch—the heart of Mark's Gospel, Mark 8:22–10:52) shown in the illustration in this chapter. At the tip of the arch, we see that Mark began with **the healing of the blind man** (8:22-26) and ended with **the healing of the deaf man** (10:46-52). Perhaps this was Mark's way of saying to his listeners: let those who have eyes see and those who have ears hear! Next on the left side of the arch comes Peter's sudden insight: Jesus, you are the Christ!

The middle of the tip of the arch has three parallel subsections. The author repeated his most important material three times in three slightly different ways—a good technique to use when people are listening to you and trying to remember what you are saying!

The top strand is found in chapter 8; the middle strand in chapter 9; and the bottom strand in chapter 10. If we look at the "slices" of the arch, we find that Mark had Jesus talking about his suffering and coming death and Resurrection three different times. Scholars call these sections the three predictions of the Passion (told in actuality in 14:1–16:8).

In the middle "slice" of the arch, we find that each time Jesus talked about what would happen to him, the disciples misunderstood somehow.

Finally in the third "slice," Jesus responded each time to their misunderstanding by teaching them about the meaning of discipleship.

Does this structure of Mark make sense to you? What questions or insights do you have?

9

Mark
11:1—12:44

In the Temple

Again, keep in mind your class of learners and how they best learn. If students are not reading the passage in their Bibles and writing out answers to the Dimension 1 questions at home before class, suggest that they read the passage and answer the questions when they first come into the classroom. Other activities can be offered to students who have already completed the questions. Other choices may include activities (A), (B), (C), (D), and (G).

Opening Prayer

Amazing God, you who are within us, beside us, and ever beyond us, we praise you in our daily lives as well as in our Sunday worship places. We confess that we struggle again and again to understand your amazing message and your never-failing offer of grace. Help us to give up our need for the security and the magic of rules, rituals, and proper worship that only seem to offer us a place within the circle of your arms. Deep in our hearts we know that all that you require is love of you and love of our neighbor. These are the hardest commands of all. Help us, God, as we continue our journey toward discipleship. In the name of Jesus, whom we seek to follow, Amen.

Dimension 1:
What Does the Bible Say?

(A) Continue to map Jesus' journey.

- Once again track Jesus' journey on your class map. Use the information below for your map study.
—Mark 11:1. Coming from Jericho, Jesus first reached Bethany, about two miles from Jerusalem, and then Bethphage, a half-mile from Jerusalem. Both are villages on the slopes of the Mount of Olives.
—Mark 11:11. Jesus entered Jerusalem, and then went back out to Bethany for the night.
—Mark 11:12. Jesus went back to Jerusalem for the day.
—Mark 11:19. Jesus went out of the city to a place not named.
—Mark 11:27. Jesus went back into Jerusalem for the third time.

(B) Look at Mark's big picture.

- If the group is large, divide into smaller groups for this activity.
- Provide a variety of commentaries for groups to use.
- Research in commentaries to discover the basic outline of the story of Jesus' ministry in Jerusalem. Ask students to prepare a short report to share in activity (F).

(C) Compare fig tree stories.

- Provide copies of Gospel parallels to use to compare Mark and Matthew's version of the withered fig tree (Mark 11:12-14 and 11:20-25; Matthew 21:18-19 and 20-22).
- Read Luke 13:6-9, another story of a fig tree.
- Again research commentaries to see what scholars say about the meanings of these stories.
- Share insights gathered through research in class.

(D) Research information on the Temple.

- Research Bible dictionaries and commentaries regarding the significance of the Temple in Jesus' day.
- Report findings to the entire class. Additional information about the Temple is found in session 10, pages 48-52.

(E) Review questions in the study book.

- Give students time in class to complete answers in their study books if they have not already done so; then briefly review the questions and answers:

    1. Jesus said that they should give to the emperor the things due the emperor.

    2. Jesus said the Sadducees were wrong to deny the resurrection. Further, he said that the risen life is qualitatively different from one's earthly life.

    3. The scribe asked Jesus which commandment is foremost among the commandments.

    4. Jesus answered that one is to love God totally and love one's neighbor as one would love oneself.

    5. The scribe responded that loving God and neighbor was far more important than offering burnt offerings or sacrifices.

- Move to activity (F) for more discussion of these stories.

(F) Discuss meanings of Mark 12:13-34.

- Ask students to give their report that they prepared in activity (B) on the larger outline of Jesus' ministry in Jerusalem.
- Summarize the major points Mark made in chapters 11 and 12. (See the study book, Dimension 2 and the sidebar on the Jerusalem Temple, pages 71-72.)
- Guide students to use Bibles and material from Dimension 2 in the study book to answer the following questions. If the class is large, divide it into teams to work on the questions.
—Why did Jesus bring "the things that are God's" into the question of whether taxes should be paid to the emperor (Mark 12:13-17)?
—What do you think is the meaning of the two answers that Jesus gave to the Sadducees' question about the resurrection (Mark 12:18-27)?
—How might the perceptive scribe have gotten any closer to the kingdom of God (Mark 12:28-34)?

(G) Sing Scripture.

- Discuss the text of hymns based on these Mark Scripture passages. Then sing them together. Possible hymns to use for this activity could include the following from *The United Methodist Hymnal*: "Tell Me the Stories of Jesus" (No. 277); "Hosanna, Loud Hosanna" (No. 278); "Mantos y Palmas" (No. 279); "All Glory, Laud, and Honor" (No. 280).
- Compare the hymn texts with the story in Mark 11:1-11.
—Do the songs accurately portray the meaning of that ride into Jerusalem, as you understand it?
—If not, how might you rewrite one of the hymns?

(H) Dramatically read the parable of the wicked tenants.

- Invite students to get into a comfortable position, close their eyes if they wish, and take several deep slow breaths to center themselves. Invite the class to "take in the story" with all their senses: sight, smell, touch, hearing, and taste.
- Read slowly, expressively, and dramatically Mark 12:1b-11.
- Discuss the following questions:
—Who is the owner of the vineyard? (God)
—Who are the tenants? (Israel)
—Who are the slaves? (perhaps Moses or the prophets)

—Who is the beloved son? (Jesus)

—What does Mark seem to be saying the meaning of this allegory is?

- Move to activity (I) in Dimension 3 to continue exploring this story.

Dimension 3:
What Does the Bible Mean to Us?

(I) Explore modern meanings of the vineyard story.

- Move from discussing the meaning of this story for Mark and Mark's listeners/readers to a discussion of the meaning for us today.
- Ask the following questions to the group:

—For us, who are the "tenants" of the vineyard?

—For us, who are the "slaves" sent by the vineyard owner?

> **TEACHING TIP**
>
> The temptation of the class may be to label modern Jews as the tenants and modern Christians like themselves (or maybe Christian missionaries or television evangelists or great preachers) as the slaves sent by the owner. Push the discussion further by asking the following questions:
>
> —How are we like the tenants?
>
> —How is the church at large like the tenant?
>
> —If the established Christian church is the tenant, who are the slaves?
>
> —If we substitute the word *slave* with the word *oppressed one*, who are the slaves sent by the vineyard owner (God) to the tenants?

(J) Write a modern allegory of the vineyard.

- Share the allegory, "A Twentieth Century Vineyard Allegory," found in the section, Additional Bible Helps, at the end of this session.
- Ask the class individually or in pairs to create their own modern allegories. Provide time for several to share their stories.

(K) Continue writing a modern gospel.

- Focus on how to tell contemporaries about the controversies Jesus had with leaders of the established Jewish religion of his time.
- Think about the following question:

—Will you use any modern analogies to help get your story across to non-Christian persons today?

(L) Write in your journals.

- Write the following question on chalkboard or newsprint so that everyone can see it: If resurrection is not resurrection of the body, what else might resurrection mean?
- Refer students to Mark 12:18-27.
- Invite students to reflect on this question and the Scripture reference as they write in their journals.
- Provide time for a brief sharing of ideas (if anyone is willing to share from their journals) or go to activity (M) below.

(M) Write a cinquain poem.

- Write a cinquain poem on the theme of resurrection.
- Make the word *resurrection* either the first line or the last line.
- Provide plain white typing paper and colored markers.
- Encourage students to turn the paper sideways and "print big." Invite them to sign their names if they wish.
- Mount finished poems on nine-by-twelve colored construction paper to provide a colored border.

> ### What Is a Cinquain?
> A cinquain (sing-CANE) poem is a French term for a five-line stanza that has a very specific structure as follows:
> Line 1   Title (a noun; one word)
> Line 2   Describes the title (two words)
> Line 3   Contains action words (verbs) or a phrase about the title (three words)
> Line 4   Describes a feeling about the title (four words)
> Line 5   A word that means the same as the title (one word)
>
> Sample Cinquain:
> > Spirit
> > within, beyond
> > sustaining my life
> > wind blowing me free
> > God

(N) Paint an impression of discipleship.

- Invite students to use large (eleven-by-seventeen inch) white drawing paper and paints to create their impression of what *discipleship* means if all of life ultimately belongs to God.
- Refer students to Mark 12:13-17 and to Dimension 2 and 3 material in their study books, pages 73-76, on the issue of what belongs to Caesar and what belongs to God. Ask them to consider the following questions:

—How do we symbolize the idea of all the world belonging to God?

—How do we symbolize discipleship in such a world?

Closing Prayer

Eternal, ever-loving God, Creator of all the world, we begin to see that your ways are not necessarily our ways. We are too often tied to the customs and traditions with which we practice our religion—and too seldom are able to respond to you in total trust and total love and adoration. God, that second part of your commandment—to love our neighbor as ourselves—that one often trips us up. We can hardly comprehend that the whole world is yours and therefore the whole world is our neighbor. Help us to keep our hearts and minds open to your ways, even when and especially when, it conflicts with our ways. Amen.

Additional Bible Helps

A Twentieth Century Vineyard Allegory

One day a person bought a large chain of newspapers that was distributed across the nation. This new owner reorganized the staffs, set up new policies of solid news reporting, and created new designs and formats for the newspapers. A new logo was chosen: Open Arms. A new creed was chosen: Love your Creator with all your heart, mind, soul, and strength—and your neighbor as yourself. The owner also created an advisory board of directors to watch over the whole chain of newspapers. Finally, before leaving the country on other business, the owner hired managing editors for each newspaper and put them in complete charge. Several years passed, and the owner who was still away began to notice that the new policies were not being fairly administered; the news was biased and exclusive; ideas that had been sent by various messengers were distorted. Reporters did not seem to be following their new creed. Furthermore, the papers seemed to be written according to an intricate set of guidelines because no deviation was ever evident.

So the owner sent an outsider—a non-newsperson academician—as a messenger to the Board of Directors; the Board refused to even see the messenger. Then the owner sent another outsider, an outspoken prophet of newspaper changes who worked for one of the alternate presses, but the editors beat the prophet to death. Again, the owner sent another outsider—this time one of the oppressed people on the streets who read the papers, then used them to keep warm. But the staffs of the newspapers just kicked that messenger out on the street.

Again, and again, the owner sent outsiders—writers, editors, and owners of alternate presses; minorities, women, and children; people living a wide range of lifestyles—with the critical message; but the hearts of the owner's employees were hardened. They killed the messengers, or wrote scathing editorials with so much misinformation in them that the messengers were ridiculed, threatened, harassed, and beaten into submission.

Finally, the owner said, "My beloved child understands what I want done; I will send this child to the employees and Board of Directors of my newspaper chain. They will listen to my child."

But they quickly set a trap. Working with the government, the Board managed to quietly have the child killed in a demonstration that got out of hand. Then the editors ran damning editorials against the teachings of the child for weeks and months and years until all vestiges of the message of the owner and child had been eradicated from the readers' minds.

Now the newspaper owner was greatly grieved at the actions of these trusted employees and vowed to give the newspaper to others who would listen and understand the message and the way of life the owner wanted to offer through the newspaper. Have you not read this Scripture?

> The stone that the builders rejected
>   has become the chief cornerstone.
> This is God's doing;
>   it is marvelous in our eyes. (Psalm 118:22-23)

The Evolution of the Temple

Remember the story of Moses? Confronted by a burning bush, Moses was told to remove his shoes. "Then he said, 'Come no closer! Remove the sandals from your feet, for the place on which you are standing is holy ground.'"

Today, when one visits the Temple mount area in Jerusalem, one quickly understands that one stands on holy soil. Like Moses, one removes one's shoes. Although the elaborate structures that once graced the site no longer stand, the soil itself is pregnant with sacred meaning. From the onset of the monarchy to the destruction of Jerusalem in A.D. 70, the Temple was the focus of Jewish culture. Like the tabernacle before it, the Temple was a vivid reminder of God's relationship with the covenant people. Not unlike buildings of our own day, the Temple seems to have "evolved" from humble beginnings to more elaborate structures.

Additional information about the Temple era may be found under the entry "Temple" in *The Oxford Companion to the Bible*, edited by Bruce M. Metzger and Michael D. Coogan (Oxford University Press, 1993), pages 731-34, or under the entry "The Temple" in *Harper's Bible Dictionary*, edited by Paul J. Achtemeier (HarperCollins Publishers, 1985), pages 1021-1029.

The Tabernacle of the Exodus

From the time of Moses until King David, the tabernacle served as the center of Jewish worship (2 Samuel 6:17; 7:6). Scripture tells us that the tabernacle was portable. Constructed under Moses by the Jewish people during the Exodus experience, the tabernacle was essentially a tent—easily erected, dismantled, and moved from one site to another. The holy of holies housed the ark of the covenant. The tabernacle befitted the nomadic ways of the Hebrew children wandering from place to place. However, over time, the Jews became less nomadic, more settled and more interested in a permanent sanctuary.

Solomon's Temple

King David planned to build a permanent worship arena, but God forbade it (1 Chronicles 12:7--8). The singular honor of building the Temple fell to King Solomon, who drew upon his father's plans and previously collected materials for the project. Located where the Moslem Dome of the Rock is located today, the original Temple resembled the tabernacle—a very lavish, permanent tabernacle! Rectangular in shape, with an inner sanctuary or holy of holies, the building boasted hollow, bronze columns and interior walls of Lebanon cedar (1 Kings 5:6-10; 6:15-16). Skilled artisans lined the structure in gold (22). Gold gilded massive olive wood doors separated the holy of holies from the nave (31). Two outer courts in the arena were for ritual sacrifice. Grand and glorious, the first Temple was destroyed by Nebuchadrezzar in 587/586 B.C. (2 Kings 25:8-17).

Zerubbabel's Temple

Following the exile experience, around 538 B.C., work began on the second Temple. About 515 B.C., the project was finished. The second Temple resembled both the tabernacle and first Temple in its design. The holy of holies and interior sanctuary were, once again, surrounded by two courts: the interior court provided for burnt offerings.

Herod's Temple

Under the direction of Herod, a third Temple was constructed between 20-18 B.C. Work continued for several years, however, on the Temple platform. The second Temple was not destroyed, as its predecessor was—it was simply rebuilt, as routine sacrifices and other Temple functions were carried out amidst the construction. The first-century historian, Josephus, wrote of Herod's project in detail.

Why would Herod, a Roman puppet-king want to refurbish a Jewish landmark? Perhaps because he coveted making Israel a significant addition to the Roman Empire. Herod's building projects may have been designed to garner public approval. Influenced by Greek and Roman architectural design, Herod's Temple displayed monumental gates and collonades. The largest and most grand of all the temples, Herod's Temple was destroyed when Jerusalem was destroyed by Roman legions in A.D. 70. Rome added insult to injury when the destruction of the Temple occurred on the same date chosen for the burning of the first Temple by the King of Babylon—the tenth day of the fifth month. Begun in splendor—rich in sacred history—the Temple era ended amid flames.

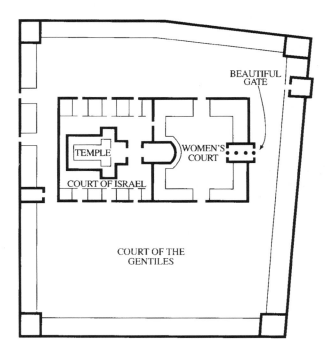

Mark
13:1-37

LEARNING MENU

Keeping in mind the ways in which your class members learn best as well as their needs and interests, choose at least one learning segment from each of the three Dimensions. Activities (A), (B), and (C) may be offered as students arrive. Consider doing activity (G) as an initial total group activity, before doing other Dimension 2 and 3 activities.

Opening Prayer

O God, be with us in our study today, for your Word is hard to understand. For some of us it may seem irrelevant to our twentieth century lives. Help us to keep our hearts and minds open to the Living Word. Within those long ago spoken and written words, Jesus urged us to "keep awake," but we are not sure we understand what that really means for us. Help us to gain deeper insight into this passage. Help us to see the bigger picture of Mark's message to his first readers and to us. In the name of the Christ, Amen.

Dimension 1:
What Does the Bible Say?

(A) Locate the Temple on a map of Jerusalem.

Locate the Temple in Jerusalem and the Mount of Olives to the east of the Temple. See the map on page 71 of the study book.

(B) Add to the timeline.

● Again provide commentaries, Bible dictionaries, and other reference books for students to use. Divide into smaller groups if the total group is large.
● Research the questions:
—When and why was the Temple in Jerusalem destroyed?
—Why was its fall so important?
● Add the date of the destruction of the Temple (A.D. 70) to the timeline that you have been working on throughout this study.
● Ask the groups to prepare a report on their research to give to the total group in activity (E).

(C) Review questions in the study book.

- While others are doing research, provide time for students who have not done so to answer questions in their study book. Answers to the questions in the study book are as follows:

1. Jesus had been teaching in the Temple in his last days in Jerusalem. He was sitting with the disciples on the Mount of Olives across from that Temple. They commented on the massiveness and extensiveness and beauty of the Temple. Jesus responded with a prediction that it would be totally destroyed.

2. The lesson to be learned from the parable of the fig tree is that when the leaves come forth, summer is upon you. Thus it will be with the end of the age: when the things described take place, the end will be immediately upon you. There will be no passage of time, just a "two-minute" warning!

3. God alone knows when the present things will pass away. Not even Jesus knows, so Mark was telling his readers that they certainly cannot know.

4. Jesus ended his teaching in chapter 13 with a parable of a man who went on a journey, leaving his slaves with tasks to do and a guard to watch the door.

(D) Ask the scholars.

- Divide the class into five teams. Pose the following questions for research, giving one question to each team.
—What was the immediate situation of Mark's first readers/listeners in approximately A.D. 64-75? (To research this question, look up "persecution times in the New Testament" in a Bible dictionary. Also check commentaries for descriptions of first century realities. See the short description in the Additional Bible Helps section of this lesson.)
—How is Mark 13 like apocalyptic literature? What does it lack to be true apocalyptic literature? (Read about apocalyptic literature in Bible dictionaries. See also the sidebar "Biblical Apocalypticism" in the study book, page 79, and the article "Apocalyptic Literature: Mystery With Meaning" from the *Bible Teacher Kit* (Abingdon, 1994), pages 71-74.
—How is Mark 13 like farewell discourses of great biblical leaders? (See the study book sidebar, "Farewell Discourses"; also read Genesis 49:2-27; Deuteronomy 32; 1 Chronicles 28; John 14—17; Acts 20:17-38.)

—What is the meaning of the parable of the fig tree? (See the study book, page 82.)
—What is the meaning of the parable of the man who goes on a journey? (Bible commentaries and dictionaries will be helpful in research here.)

Dimension 2: What Does the Bible Mean?

(E) Read the Scripture expressively.

- Select a group member who reads especially well to read the entire Mark 13 passage to the rest of the group. Assign the reading ahead of time in order to give the reader time to practice reading the Scripture as expressively as possible.
- Ask for the groups who participated in activity (B) to report on their findings to the questions they researched. After hearing the various reports, ask students to listen to the Mark 13 passage read expressively. Invite them to listen as if they were a first century Christian. Invite comments about insights, feelings, and concerns they had while listening.

(F) Explore the basic meanings of Mark 13.

- Pose the following discussion questions to the total group:
—Obviously, the "end of the age" did not happen in Jesus' generation; what did happen?
—What changes occurred?
—Did an "age" end somehow?
—Was Jesus wrong?

Dimension 3: What Does the Bible Mean to Us?

(G) Discuss "endings" in our lives.

- Have available a chalkboard or newsprint available to use with this activity.
- Ask students to jot down on paper all the various "endings" (personal and social/global) that have occurred in and during their lifetime.

- On chalkboard make two lists in columns. Title one list "Personal Endings" and the other list "Social/Global Endings."
- Ask students to contribute to the chalkboard list endings from their personal lists that they feel comfortable in sharing with the group, recognizing that some endings may be too personal to share. Possible endings might include such events as the following: left home; graduated from college; end of Vietnam War; breakup of the Soviet Union; a divorce; a death.
- Discuss the following questions:
—What was happening before the endings? (signs of something new? troubles? false statements? or proclamations?)
—What happened after the endings?
—Which endings might be said to be "the end of an age"?

(H) Continue writing a modern gospel.

- Remind the group that Mark's first readers were living in an era and among people who expected the "end of the current age" and the coming of a "new age" that would be ushered in by the coming again of Jesus.
- Ask the groups to consider the following questions:
—What do you think is the overarching "worldview" today for Christians and non-Christians?
—What kind of chapter 13 would you write in your modern gospel to these modern people?
—What would be your main points, your one primary message?

(I) Write a cinquain poem.

- Refer to the sidebar, "What Is a Cinquain?" found on page 45.
- Review for the students the structure for the five-line stanzas.
- Suggest that they use the word *Endings* as either the first or last word of their poem.
- Provide materials for mounting the poems and displaying on a wall in the classroom.
- Provide time for reading aloud some of the poems, perhaps just before the closing prayer.

> Endings
> last things
> turning things around
> dying a thousand deaths
> Beginnings

(J) Continue journaling.

- Ask students to continue journaling by exploring their thoughts on the major question: How would you describe your belief that God will ultimately rule in a "new age"?

- Ask them to consider these sub-questions:
—Do you project an end of all history (believing that the church has so disobeyed that God must step outside of history to correct things)?
—Do you foresee a radical revolution in history (in the church/in the world) after which the command to love God and love neighbor as self prevails?
—What kinds of signs, false prophets, and tribulations might we have in our twentieth century world/universe?
—What is your/our task in the meantime? (The answer may be to watch and to proclaim the good news.)

(K) Discuss meanings for us today.

- Explore as a total group the major ideas expressed in Dimension 3 of the study book. Use the questions below as starters.
- If the class is large and time is short, divide the group into pairs and give each pair a list of the questions (or print all the questions on newsprint).
—What does the writer of the study book mean by his statement that Christian apocalypticism (and thus Mark 13) "has built into it a faith with size and a scope as vast as all creation"?
—What for you are the major motifs or elements of the story of Jesus that cannot be left out and still be the Christian message?
—What does it mean that God will ultimately triumph?
—Does radical evil require an apocalyptic view? Would a radical evolutionary or revolutionary view work?
—Do you think we are so condemned as a church and a world that God must ultimately step into history and end it to create God's kingdom? Or do you think that God always acts *within history*?

(L) Sing Scripture.

- Use copies of hymnals to find hymns that have texts about the end of the age or "new heaven/new earth" imagery. Some examples might include the following: "Lo, He Comes with Clouds Descending," (*The United*

Methodist Hymnal, No. 718), "Battle Hymn of the Republic," (No. 717), and "My Lord, What a Morning" (No. 719), and "Awake, Awake to Love and Work," (*Methodist Hymnal*, 1964; page 190).

- Compare the messages of these hymns.
- Ask students which hymn they feel best portrays their understanding of Mark's message in chapter 13.

(M) Explore discipleship in word and art.

- Provide drawing paper, paint, crayons, and/or felt-tip markers for this activity.
- Remind students that whether or not we believe in the return of Jesus and the end of history as we know it, part of chapter 13 is a message of what we are to do in the meantime. What we are to do is to proclaim the good news to all nations (Mark 13:10). This Scripture has served as a foundation for Christian missionary work around the world.
- Ask students to consider the following questions:
—Given our growing understandings of diversity and our recognition of other people's religious beliefs, how are we to understand this command?
—What does it mean to "proclaim" and what is the good news to be proclaimed in the late twentieth century?
- After initial discussion about this issue, invite students to use paint, crayons, or felt-tip markers to do a "then and now" interpretation of this command by dividing their drawing paper in half and creating a first century image or symbol on one half of the page and a twentieth century image or symbol on the other half.
- Invite students to comment on their drawings if they wish.

(N) Identify Jesus' major points.

- Ask students to think about their daily readings suggested in Dimension 4 of the study book.
- If you have a small class, give each student newsprint to print out the major points they found in these daily readings. Hang these on the wall and spend a little time just reading them silently.
- Discuss these questions:
—Where do we all agree on Jesus' message?
—Where do we disagree?
—If we had to condense the points to one major message, what would it be?

TEACHING TIP
Give students time to come to a common agreement if they can about the single basic message. If they cannot come to one statement, acknowledge that basic diversity exists sometimes in the way we as Christians understand the Bible.

- A possible line of thinking might be as follows:
—Do not be lead astray.
—Do not be alarmed.
—Keep preaching the good news even if you are persecuted.
—Have faith. God will cut short the days of suffering.
—Be alert. I have told you everything already.
—Keep awake. You do not know when these things will happen; only God knows.
—The one primary message: Never mind the end or when it is coming; you are called to be alert and to proclaim the good news to the world.

Closing Prayer
Ever-loving, ever-mysterious, magnificent and gracious God, we continue to sort out our beliefs, opinions, customs, and traditions. We seek clarity of what it truly means to be a disciple of the Christ. We do not all agree, and we are trying to be accepting of each other's beliefs and opinions, while always inviting each other into deeper understandings and insights. We would be your faithful people. Amen.

Additional Bible Helps

The Temple in Jerusalem
Three successive Jewish Temples were built in Jerusalem in biblical time. The first Temple was Solomon's, which was begun in 961 B.C. and finished seven years later. It is

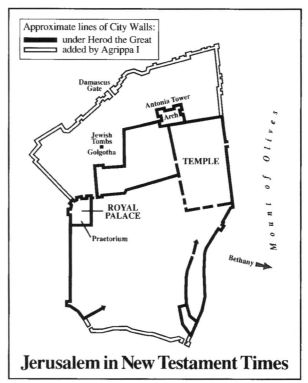

Jerusalem in New Testament Times

described in 1 Kings 5—8. Solomon continued for thirteen more years to build palaces and other royal buildings adjacent to the Temple, thus creating a "royal chapel." The Temple gained in public and national significance as the story of the Hebrew people continued. Over several centuries it was plundered and then finally burned in 587/586 B.C.

Zerubbabel's Temple was the second Temple. It was begun sometime during the post-exile period (after 539 B.C.) on the same site, and probably finished in 516/515 B.C. This second Temple stood for nearly five hundred years as a center of Jewish religion.

The third Temple was Herod's. He began to dismantle the second Temple about 20 B.C. in order to build his new one. Its basic structure was finished in about eighteen months, but work continued for a half a century. It was destroyed in A.D. 70, about the time that the Book of Mark was probably written.

Today a famous Muslim shrine known as the Dome of the Rock is built on the site.

First Century New Testament Realities
In the first century experience of early Christians, such as those first listening to or reading Mark's Gospel, persecution was a reality. In their experience was probably the physical horrors of persecution by Nero in A.D. 64 along with civil chaos that followed in the later years of his reign to his death in A.D. 68.

The Roman historian Tacitus (A.D. 56-116) tells us that early Christians, out of jealousy and discord within their own community, ended up accusing each other during those persecution times.

11

Mark 14:1-72

WHAT IS YOUR DECISION?

Opening Prayer
Compassionate, giving God, open our hearts and minds once again to the continuing story of Jesus, a true child of humanity and thus a true child of yours. Help us to risk looking at ourselves and how we act as false witnesses, or persecutors. Help us to remember that even though we are finite human beings and never perfect or worthy, you still offer all of us unlimited love and forgiveness. In the name of the One who was falsely accused, Amen.

Dimension 1:
What Does the Bible Say?

(A) Map Jesus' movements in Jerusalem.

- Using a map of Jerusalem (see the map, page 51), continue to trace Jesus' movements by marking them with yarn. In Mark 13 we left Jesus at the Mount of Olives across from the Temple in Jerusalem.

His movements in chapter 14 are as follows:
—Mark 14:3. Jesus was at Bethany outside Jerusalem staying with Simon the leper who was otherwise unknown. This would have startled Mark's readers; again Jesus was associating with outsiders. See John 12:1-2 where John has Mark staying at the home of Mary, Martha, and Lazarus.
—Mark 14:13. Jesus was within the city of Jerusalem celebrating Passover.
—Mark 14:26. Jesus went to the Mount of Olives.
—Mark 14:32. Jesus moved to a place called Gethsemane on the Mount of Olives. Look up Gethsemane in a Bible dictionary.
—Mark 14:53. Jesus was in the presence of the high priest at an unknown place in the city of Jerusalem.

(B) Review questions in the study book.

- While others are doing research, provide time for students who have not done so to answer questions in their study book. Answers to the questions in the study book are as follows:
1. The sequence of the story of Peter's denials are as follows: a servant girl identified Peter with Jesus; Peter denied Jesus; the cock crowed; the servant girl identified Peter to bystanders as "one of them"; Peter denied it; a

bystander identified Peter as a follower, a Galilean; Peter denied Jesus; the cock crowed a second time. Mark had thus once again shown his first readers/listeners that Jesus was a true prophet.

2. The high priest, all the chief priests, the elders, and the scribes were present at the trial, which was a Jewish assembly. Jesus and the witnesses against him were also there.

3. Jesus was condemned by the Jewish authorities after he answered the high priest that he was indeed the Messiah. The priest claimed this was blasphemy, apparently based on Leviticus 24:16.

(C) Compare Gospel accounts of Judas' betrayal.

● Provide copies of a Gospel parallel for Mark 14:10-11 and 14:17-21. Also look up John 13:21-30. Look for differences among the four stories.

TEACHING TIP

One way to compare the four Gospels is to have one person read aloud Mark 14 while others follow along in the comparable passages from Matthew, Luke, and John. When a difference is noted, stop so that everyone in the group can hear the difference. Then continue reading and watching for further differences. Discuss whether or not the differences seem major or minor.

Dimension 2: What Does the Bible Mean?

(D) Ask the scholars about Passover.

● Check commentaries and Bible dictionaries to answer the following questions:
—What is the Festival of the Passover and the Feast of the Unleavened Bread?
—What do scholars think were the earliest verses and forms of this chapter? (See the study book, page 88, for a theory on the early development of this chapter and sources Mark may have had available to him.)

(E) Discuss meanings of Mark 14.

● Pose the following questions to the group. Use the Dimension 2 material and boxed information in the study book, pages 87-91, along with suggested commentaries for answers.

—How is the description of the Last Supper like the feeding of the five thousand (6:30-44) or the four thousand (8:1-10)? How is it different? (*The Harper's Bible Commentary, page 1004, notes that the language is similar to the earlier passages; now Jesus feeds the disciples and declares himself to be the bread and wine for them. Scholars speculate that this was one of the earliest fragments of this chapter, and probably was developed for use in the liturgy and worship of the early church.*)
—In what sense did Peter speak the truth about not knowing Jesus?
—Did Peter show Jesus to be a true or false prophet?
—How did Peter's denial and Jesus' answer and behavior at the trial demonstrate an earlier teaching of Jesus about saving your life and losing it (Mark 8:34-38)?
—Who was really on trial that night?
—How did Mark's view of the Twelve continue to be one of disgust?
—In contrast, how did the woman who anointed Jesus exhibit faithfulness? (One interpretation understands that the woman symbolized faithful discipleship. Mark creates an arch or frame with this story at the beginning of the Passion and the women going to the tomb to anoint Jesus at the end of the book. The disciples (the chosen ones) symbolize human frailty: in the Passover meal they did not believe him; in the garden they could not stay awake; Judas betrayed him; the disciples deserted him at Gethsemane; Peter denied him in the courtyard of the high priest.)

(F) Consider the theme of secrecy.

● Look back at how Mark employed a writing technique almost like a mystery story, thus keeping Jesus' true identity secret.
● See the sidebar article in the study book, pages 55-56, on the theme of secrecy.
● Open discussion in the group on the following question.
—How did Mark *partially end* his whole secrecy technique during the telling of the trial?

(G) Relate Jesus' trial to the parable of the sower.

● Review the parable of the sower (Mark 4:3-8) by reading it expressively to the class or ask another class member to do so.
● Discuss the questions in the What to Watch For section at the beginning of the chapter in the study book (pages 86-87).

(H) Experience the arrest and trial.

- Gather several large teaching pictures (a good source is from older children's curriculum) that show Jesus in the Garden of Gethsemane, the sleeping disciples, the betrayal of Judas with a kiss, the disciples deserting, and the trial before the Jewish leaders.
- Hang these pictures in sequence so that class members can sit and meditate on them.
- Use the following reflective meditation:
  Find a comfortable position so that you can see all of the pictures . . . . Take several deep breaths and exhale slowly and evenly after each . . . . Let your eyes wander over the pictures . . . . Take in the scenes . . . how the people looked . . . that it is nighttime . . . . Feel the darkness surrounding you . . . . You are sitting on a hill outside the city . . . overlooking the Temple . . . . You can see the outlines in the darkness . . . feel the breezes . . . look up at the stars . . . . You are waiting . . . for Jesus has gone ahead with Peter, James, and John . . . and you are getting very sleepy . . . . Your eyes keep closing . . . . Your body relaxes . . . "Simon, are you asleep? Could you not keep awake one hour? Stay awake and pray that you may not come into the time of trial" . . . and you try . . . but you are sleepy . . . and the tension of the week has caught up with you . . . . Whatever can Jesus mean by his words? . . .

  "Are you still sleeping? Enough! The hour has come . . . See my betrayer is at hand" . . . .

  Suddenly you are wide awake! Judas moves toward Jesus and kisses him and immediately soldiers surround Jesus with swords drawn . . . . You slowly back away . . . and then you turn and run. But not far! You follow as they take Jesus to the house of the high priest . . . . You cautiously walk into the courtyard . . . and warm yourself by a fire . . . . "No, no, I do not know or understand what you are talking about" . . . .

  What will they do to me if they find out I have been following Jesus? . . . In the distance, the cock crows . . . . "No, I tell you I do not know Jesus" . . . . They might seize me and beat me . . . .

  "This man is one of them."

  "No, I swear I do not know this man you are talking about" . . . and the cock crows again!

  In the muffled time of early morning . . . are hurled the accusations: "This one says he'll destroy our Temple and build it again in three days! . . . in the distance through the building . . . comes the mocking voice: "Are you the Messiah, the Son of the Blessed

  One?" . . . and the faint answer stirs on the breeze: "I am."

  (Longer pause for reflection)

  Come back into the present to discuss the experience.
- Pose the following questions one at a time to the class. Invite their reflections.
—What was your major experience during the reflection time? your major feelings?
—How (or when) are we like the disciples at the time of the arrest?
—How (or when) are we like Judas?
—How (or when) are we like Peter in the courtyard?
—How (or when) are we like the high priest?
—How (or when) are we like the witnesses at the trial?
—How (or when) is the church today like Peter, or Judas, or the witnesses, or the high priest?

(I) Conduct a modern trial of Jesus.

- Assign roles to students.
- Those who are against Jesus: a DISTRICT SUPER-INTENDENT; a LOCAL CHURCH PASTOR; a LOCAL CHURCH LAYMAN; a BIBLICAL SCHOLAR; WITNESS 1 (someone who thinks Jesus' miracles are evidence of witchcraft); WITNESS 2 (someone who thinks Jesus' teaching against long-held religious customs and laws will split the denominational church in two); WITNESS 3 (someone who thinks Jesus broke a lot of religious customs by associating with various outcasts of our century—the homeless, the mentally ill, outspoken feminist women, gay men with AIDS, unmarried teen mothers, African Americans, Native Americans, Latinos, and lesbians).
- Those who support Jesus: a DISTRICT SUPERINTENDENT; a BIBLICAL SCHOLAR; a LOCAL CHURCH PASTOR; LAYPERSON 1 (whose life in drugs and crime was turned around by hearing about and believing in Jesus); LAYPERSON 2 (who lives on the edge of the established church, not fully acceptable); LAYPERSON 3 (who in some way has experienced a "death" and "resurrection" in her or his own life).
- Give each person time to write out a three- to five-sentence accusation against or testimony for Jesus.
- Assign the rest of the class to be the jury.
- While participants write statements, talk to the rest of the class about their role as the jury: they are to (1) listen with open minds, (2) forget anything they have ever heard about Jesus, and (3) come to a decision on Jesus' guilt or innocence after hearing all the testimony.
- Ask students to share feelings about their roles in the trial. Ask students about their insights and learnings.

(J) Write a creed.

- Look briefly at traditional creeds of the church.
- Share the modern creed for secular times by Dorothe Solle in the Additional Bible Helps at the end of this chapter.
- Invite students to write a personal creed of their own.

(K) Discuss where your loyalties lie.

- Discuss as a group the following questions:
—What claims your absolute loyalty and commitment? Is your absolute loyalty to God through obeying the great commandment or is it to something else? (See the Dimension 3 section, pages 91-92, of the study book.)
—What if God is trying once again to speak through humanity and within history—through those that many in the Christian church consider to be "outsiders" and "sinners"?
—How are *you* responding?

(L) Write in the journals.

- Sing the hymn "Are Ye Able" (*The United Methodist Hymnal*, No. 530) and the spiritual, "Lord, I Want to Be a Christian" (No. 402).
- Then ask students to write their thoughts about the following questions. Print them on newsprint and hang them so that the class can refer to them as they write:
—Are we really able to follow Jesus?
—Do we really want to be Christian if it means literally following a path to our death?
—Is this what we are called to do?
—Invite students to share from their journal writing if they wish.

(M) Continue writing a modern gospel.

- Ask groups to focus on writing a chapter for a modern gospel, considering the question: Who do people say I am?

(N) Create a banner.

- Invite students to brainstorm a way to combine the experience of "denial" and the experience of "discipleship" on a banner.
- Then begin making a banner (see the sidebar).
- To get the class started, ask these questions:
—What symbol or stylized figure form might you use for "denial"?
—What symbol or stylized form might you use for "discipleship"?
—How might you show symbolically the relationship between the two?

Making a Banner

For a cloth banner, provide a piece(s) of cloth for the background, usually in a solid color. For a paper banner, use large piece(s) of heavy paper from a roll or posterboard(s) as the background.

The background cloth or paper should be at least twice as long as it is wide (20 by 8 inches for a personal banner, or 72 by 30 inches for a large class banner).

For the designs and words, use pieces of cloth of different colors and designs, felt, yarn, string, and so forth. Encourage freeform letters to create any words needed for the banner.

Put banners together with fabric glue, white glue, or needles and thread.

Provide scissors, paper, and pencils for sketching plans.

Closing Prayer

Compassionate, ever-loving God, we know that you continue to reach out to us even as we falter and sometimes deny you, even as we sometimes bear false witness about you, even as we sometimes desert you. Forgive us and help us in our confusion and unbelief. For we continue to strive to be like Jesus. We continue to work on telling the good news about you to the world. In the name of the one who shows us the meaning of faith and the meaning of the Kingdom, Amen.

What Is Your Decision?

Who is this man Jesus? Ultimately each has to answer this question for him or herself. Here is one woman's creed for secular times:

I believe in jesus christ
who was right when he
like each of us
just another individual who couldn't beat city hall
worked to change the status quo
and was destroyed
Looking at him I see
how our intelligence is crippled
our imagination stifled
our efforts wasted
because we do not live as he did
every day I am afraid
that he died in vain
because he is buried in our churches
because we have betrayed his revolution
in our obedience to authority
and our fear of it
I believe in jesus christ
who rises again and again in our lives
so that we will be free
from prejudice and arrogance
from fear and hate
and carry on his revolution
and make way for his kingdom

From the English translation, *Revolutionary Patience*, by Dorothea Solle (Orbis, 1977). Used by permission.

12
Mark 15:1-41

*T*RULY THIS MAN WAS GOD'S SON!

Opening Prayer

God, we are coming to the close of Mark's story about Jesus. Some of us are very sure what the Crucifixion means. Others of us are still trying to sort it out. Help us to be good listeners. Help us to be tolerant of persons who have points of view that are different from ours. Help us to keep our hearts and minds open to the possibility of new insight into the old, old story and into your living word-deed. Amen.

Dimension 1:
What Does the Bible Say?

(A) Continue mapping Jesus' movements in Jerusalem.

- Talk about Jesus' movements with the group. Jesus' movements became more limited as his last week in Jerusalem came to an end. From the place of the high priest where the trial took place, he was taken to Pilate (15:1); then to the courtyard of the palace (15:16); and then to Golgotha (15:22) where he was crucified.

- Research information on the location of the following people and places in a Bible dictionary:
—Pilate
—Praetorium
—Golgotha

- Then mark the locations (or possible locations) on your map of Jerusalem.

(B) Add to the timeline.

- Add the years of the rule of Pilate (A.D. 26-36) to the timeline on the wall of your classroom if you created one in the first session.

- Reflect on the period of time surrounding Jesus' life and the writing of the Gospel of Mark.

(C) Review questions in the study book.

- If students have not answered the questions in the study book, give them an opportunity to do so now. Answers to the questions are as follows:

1. Jesus was charged with being the "King of the Jews."

58

2. The Roman soldiers taunted Jesus before he was crucified; the people who passed by and the chief priests and scribes taunted him while he hung on the cross.

3. Jesus cried out "My God, my God, why have you forsaken me?"

4. Mary Magdalene, Mary the mother of James the younger and of Joses, Salome, and other women who had followed him all along and provided for him stood at a distance from the cross. James and Joses are brothers of Jesus, so this Mary is also the mother of Jesus.

Dimension 2:
What Does the Bible Mean?

(D) Discuss the Roman trial.

- Divide the class into four teams and give each team a question listed below.
- Ask teams to research briefly the commentaries and Bible dictionaries for answers, before reporting to the whole class.
—Who was Pilate and why did the Jewish leaders turn Jesus over to Pilate? How do the other Gospels portray Pilate? Why the differences, do you think? Students may add to their research on Pilate from their work in activity (A).
—What was the meaning of the charge "King of the Jews," which was nailed above Jesus on the cross? How was this charge different from the one leveled against Jesus by the high priest in Mark 14?
—How did Jesus' answer to Pilate differ from his answer to the high priest the night before? What parallels and meanings might Mark have been sketching out for his readers? (See *Harper's Bible Commentary*, page 1007, for interpretation.)
—Who did Pilate release instead of Jesus? Why? What does the name Barabbas mean?

(E) Discuss the death and those who were witnesses.

- Lead the group in a discussion using the following questions as discussion starters:
—When people misunderstood Jesus' last words on the cross and thought he was calling to Elijah, what did they think would happen?
—How did the writer of the study book interpret Jesus' last words?
—The final focus of this death scene for Mark seems to be on the centurion (see the study book, page 99). What was significant about the centurion's statement about Jesus? (Mark's signature is coming through again: those in Mark's Gospel who saw the truth about Jesus always

came to him in faith; they did not "get" faith and then see who Jesus was. Up to now in Mark, only the heavenly voice in the Transfiguration scene and the voices of the unclean spirits had truly named Jesus. Mark seems to be saying that only at the death of Jesus was the confession appropriate.)
—The writer of the study book says that despite Jesus' feeling of abandonment on the cross, Mark showed that God was indeed present. What signs did the writer of the study book see in Mark's Gospel to support this claim?
—In Mark 15:38 we find the last of Mark's "anti-Temple" references. What is the significance of the tearing of the veil of the Temple? (See *Harper's Bible Commentary*, page 1008.)

(F) Compare Jesus' last words in the Gospels.

- Compare Jesus' last words in Mark with those of Luke 23:34-46 and John 19:30. Then compare these with Psalm 22:1.
- Read what commentators have to say about those words.
—How do they interpret the cry of abandonment?
—How does the psalm figure into their interpretations?
—Name all who have abandoned Jesus.

TEACHING TIP
Follow up on this discussion with the journaling activity (I) in Dimension 3.

Dimension 3:
What Does the Bible Mean to Us?

(G) Look at the almost invisible women and the absent men.

- Speculate on why women followers, standing at some distance from the cross, were there and not the male disciples.
—What might they have been feeling? thinking?
—Where might the men have been? Why?

TEACHING TIP
Explore not only personal feelings and reasons for the women and the men, but also look at the political realities. The men might well have been arrested along with Jesus who was basically charged with sedition (stirring up trouble and discontent with the existing government).

(H) Dramatically read the Crucifixion story.

- Locate several teaching pictures of the Crucifixion from older children's curriculum resources that show the Roman soldiers, the women standing off to the side, those passing by, religious leaders mocking Jesus, and the thieves who were crucified with Jesus.
- Group these pictures together so that the class can sit and look at them during this activity. Invite students to get comfortable, to take several slow deep breaths to center themselves, and then to "feel themselves into the pictures" as you (or another group member) read to them.
- Read Mark 15:22-39 slowly and expressively.
- Pause momentarily at the end before asking the following questions to the group who are still in a meditative state of mind:
—Where are you in these pictures? . . .
—Who are you? . . .
—How are you feeling? . . .
—What are you thinking? . . .
—What will you do now that Jesus has died? . . .
Again, ellipses (. . .) mean "pause."
- Ask students to share the feelings and internal responses they had during the reflection time.

(I) Continue to write in journals.

- Pose these questions for personal journal writing:
—When have you been like Jesus, feeling everyone and even God has abandoned you?
—What finally sustained you?
- Invite students to share from their writings if they wish, but do not push persons to share.

(J) What is the center of your faith?

- Ask students to reread the section that opens chapter 12 of the study book, What to Watch For, page 94.
- Use the discussion questions below to help sort out the issues:
—What is the center of your faith? Why?
—What does it mean that the cross is the center of Christianity?
—If the cross is not the central symbol of our faith, what is? Easter and the Resurrection? Pentecost?
—Mark has the centurion confessing Jesus as God's Son when he saw Jesus die, but does this mean that our focus should be on the cross? Might a case be made that, given all we know about Jesus and about God, our focus should be on his life and ministry?
—How could we finish this sentence: Perhaps what Jesus wanted and what God wants is for us to . . . .

TEACHING TIP

This activity builds on the activity about the centrality of the cross in session 7. Keep the discussion open-ended and nonconfrontational. Help people to listen to each other and to be tolerant of others' views. None of us has the absolute last word of truth about these things. Reassure people that letting go of some belief they have long held *does not* mean that they are losing their faith; faith grows and matures as we grow in our ability and willingness to look at what we believe and why.
NOTE: Even if you have a large class, this is probably a time to keep the group together to provide a calm role model for discussion.

(K) Finish the banner or make a new one.

- Finish the banner you started last week or create a simple one today focused on the idea of what it means to be faithful. Remember, banners are word-pictures that tell of a big idea in simple, stark images.

(L) Show a homemade video.

- If students have been working on a video using the hymn "Are Ye Able" (suggested for an earlier session), have them present it today for the class.
- After the showing, invite the class to share first their positive feelings and comments about the video; then ask for any other questions, comments, or concerns the video raised.

(M) Sing Scripture.

- Sing the African-American spiritual "Were You There" (*The United Methodist Hymnal*, No. 288). Compare the words to Mark's version of the Crucifixion.
- Now sing the hymn substituting the phrase "where were you" for the words "were you there."
- Talk about your feelings and any images that came to you as you sang the song the second time. Did any new insights about discipleship occur to you?

(N) Write a chapter for a modern gospel.

- Ask groups to continue writing a chapter for a modern gospel version about Jesus' last days in Jerusalem through the trials.
- Encourage groups to focus on the question:
—What will you say to contemporary people about the controversy with religious authorities, the larger political scene with the Romans, and the way the people in Jerusalem responded to Pilate?

Closing Prayer

Loving and sustaining God, we praise you for all that you have given to us. We give thanks for the life-giving story of Jesus who tried to live out your Kingdom here among us. Those old, old stories of Jesus touch our lives in a way that no other stories do. We offer you our complete trust as Jesus taught us to do. Give us courage to look again and again at our beliefs, to make them stronger and clearer and more in tune with your will and your ways. Amen.

Additional Bible Helps

What Each Gospel Says About Jesus' Crucifixion

MARK	Matthew	Luke	John
			The soldiers mock Jesus (19:1-3).
Pilate sentences Jesus to death (15:6-15).	Pilate sentences Jesus to death (27:15-26).	Pilate sentences Jesus to death (23:31-25).	Pilate sentences Jesus to death (19:4-16).
The soldiers mock Jesus (15:16-20).	The soldiers mock Jesus (27:27-31).		
Simon of Cyrene carries Jesus' cross (15:21).	Simon of Cyrene carries Jesus' cross (27:32).	Simon of Cyrene carries Jesus' cross (23:26).	Jesus carries his cross by himself (19:17a).
		Jesus speaks to women of Jerusalem (23:27-31).	
Jesus is crucified at Golgotha at nine o'clock in the morning. Jesus refuses to drink wine mixed with myrrh. The soldiers divide Jesus' clothing by casting lots. (15:22-25)	Jesus is crucified at Golgotha. Jesus refuses to drink wine mixed with gall. The soldiers divide Jesus' clothing by casting lots. (27:32-36)	Jesus is crucified at the place called "The Skull." The soldiers divide Jesus' clothing by casting lots. The soldiers offer Jesus sour wine. (23:33, 34b, 36)	Jesus is crucified at Golgotha. The soldiers divide Jesus' clothing by casting lots. (19:17b-18a, 23-25a)
Jesus' charge reads "The King of the Jews" (15:26).	Jesus' charge reads "This is Jesus, the King of the Jews" (27:37).	Jesus' charge reads "This is the King of the Jews" (23:38).	Jesus' charge reads "Jesus of Nazareth, the King of the Jews." Many of the Jews complain to Pilate about the inscription. (19:19-22)
Two bandits are crucified alongside Jesus (15:27-28).	Two bandits are crucified alongside Jesus (27:38).	Two bandits are crucified alongside Jesus (23:32).	Two others are crucified alongside Jesus (19:18b).
		Jesus says, "Father, forgive them; for they do not know what they are doing" (23:34a).	

What Each Gospel Says About Jesus' Crucifixion

MARK	Matthew	Luke	John
Jesus is mocked by bystanders (15:29-32).	Jesus is mocked by bystanders and the crucified bandits (27:38-44).	Jesus is mocked by bystanders and one of the crucified bandits. The other crucified bandit comes to Jesus' defense and is promised a place with Jesus in Paradise (23:35-37, 39-43).	
			Jesus speaks to his mother and to "the disciple whom he loved" (19:25-27).
Darkness falls from noon until three (15:33).	Darkness falls from noon until three (27:45).	Darkness falls from noon until three (23:44-45a).	
		The Temple curtain splits in two (23:45b).	
Jesus cries out "My God, my God, why have you forsaken me?" (15:34-36)	Jesus cries out, "My God, my God, why have you forsaken me?" (27:46-49)		
			Jesus says, "I am thirsty," and drinks a sponge of wine (19:28-29).
Jesus dies with a loud cry (15:37).	Jesus dies with a loud cry (27:50).	Jesus dies after crying with a loud voice, "Father, into your hands I commend my spirit" (23:46).	Jesus dies, saying, "It is finished" (19:30).
The Temple curtain splits in two (15:38).	The Temple curtain splits in two (27:51).		
	Tombs open and many of the saints are raised from the dead (27:52-53).		
The centurion says, "Truly this man was God's Son" (15:39).	The centurion and others say, "Truly this man was God's Son" (27:54).	The centurion praises God and says, "Certainly this man was innocent" (23:47).	

13

**Mark
15:42–16:20**

HE IS GOING AHEAD OF YOU

LEARNING MENU

Keeping in mind the ways in which your class members learn best as well as their needs and interests, choose at least one learning segment from each of the three Dimensions.

In this final session, choose activities to help students bring temporary closure to their explorations of who Jesus is, while reminding them of future studies in our journey through the Bible, and of the need to continually be open and growing in their faith.

Use activities (A), (B), (I), or (K) as class members arrive.

Opening Prayer

Dear God, we have met Jesus face to face and heard his "good news"—his message that your Kingdom, your new realm, your new earth is coming near. We have followed him along the road through his ministry in Galilee and beyond. We have journeyed with him to Jerusalem and to his trial and his death. Now we face again that empty tomb and we are asking once more: Who is this man Jesus? What is this good news? Help us, God, as we ask these questions and explore these stories. Keep our hearts and our minds open to your Living Word. Help us not to miss the point of Jesus' life and ministry because we are too

focused on our own customs and laws and traditions. In the name of the One who goes before us, leading the way and opening our eyes to the true meaning of the Kingdom, Amen.

Dimension 1:
What Does the Bible Say?

(A) Review the map of Jesus' journey.

● As students arrive ask them to look up "Joseph of Arimathea" in a Bible dictionary to discover who he was and where his tomb is thought to have been.

● As a way of bringing this map activity to conclusion, place three small signs on appropriate areas of the map(s): Galilean ministry, journey to Jerusalem, and last days.

● Discuss the following questions as members complete this activity:

—What general understandings about Jesus have you gained from doing this map activity?

—What general understandings about the writer of Mark and his intentions in describing the movements of Jesus have you gained from doing this map activity?

(B) Look at the endings of Mark.

- As students arrive, use an NRSV Bible to review the various endings of Mark.
- Then assign reading from the study book: "The Origins of Mark", page 5; and "The Ending of Mark's Gospel", page 105.
- Ask students to summarize findings about the endings for a report later in the session. See activity (G).

(C) Add to the timeline.

- On the wall timeline (begun in session 1) place these three dates:
—the estimated date of the Book of Mark: A.D. 65 to 75
—estimated date of the Longer Ending of Mark (16:9-20): A.D. 150-200
—estimated date of the Shorter Ending of Mark: A.D. 300 or later.

(D) Compare Gospel endings.

- Provide copies from a Gospel parallel of Mark 16:1-8.
- As a group, look for similarities and differences. Note also the footnotes to the other Gospels and the similarities and differences in those Gospels that were not included in the canon of the Bible.
- Look at commentaries to see what biblical scholars say about the endings of Matthew and Luke.
- Prepare a brief summary for presentation later in session (G).

(E) Review questions in the study book.

- If students have not answered the questions from Dimension 1 in the study book, give them time to do so now.
- The answers to the questions are as follows:
   1. Joseph of Arimathea, a member of an unnamed Jewish council, claimed Jesus body.
   2. Mary Magdalene, Mary the mother of James (Jesus' mother), and Salome came to prepare Jesus' body for burial. These same women were mentioned as standing at a distance from the cross in Mark 15.

   3. The women encountered "a young man dressed in a white robe." The clothes may have indicated to Mark's first readers that this was a heavenly messenger.
   4. The young man told them that Jesus had been raised and that his body was not there. Further, he instructed them to go tell Peter and the disciples that he was going ahead of them to Galilee; there they would see him, just as he said.
   5. The women fled in terror and amazement, and "they said nothing to anyone, for they were afraid."

Dimension 2: What Does the Bible Mean?

(F) Discuss Jesus' death and resurrection.

- Using the Dimension 2 material from chapter 13 in the study book, "The Resurrection of Jesus" (pages 103-104) and "The Ending of Mark's Gospel" (page 105), explore these questions:
—Does the Bible ever actually describe the Resurrection?
—What clues led people to assume Jesus had been resurrected?
—Who had prepared the body of Jesus for burial?
—How did Mark shift his approach to the secrecy of who Jesus was at the end of 16:8? What is the irony here?
—What is Mark's ultimate question to his readers?

(G) Why the different endings of Mark?

- Invite those who did activity (B) and (D) to report their findings to the entire class.
- Note the various dates for the endings that were added to the timeline in activity (C) or list the endings and their dates now on a newsprint or chalkboard.
- Explore these questions:
—What might be the faith reasons for those added endings of Mark?
—What might be the political reasons for those added endings?
—What case might be made for a "lost" ending of Mark that told more of what the women actually did?
—What case can be made that the ending of 16:8 is just the way Mark wanted it?
—How does it fit with the rest of the book?

(H) What do we do now?

- Divide the class into two groups: women followers and male disciples.
- Ask everyone to listen carefully to the Scriptures that you will read (Mark 14:32, 14:41-42, 14:45-50; 15:22-24; 15:40-42; 16:1-8).
- After reading the Scriptures, give each team the appropriate set of questions to answer (see the sidebars).

TEACHING TIP

Again, the point here is not to set men against women, but to explore the different experiences that women and men might have had of the events surrounding Jesus' trial, crucifixion and the empty tomb.

After each group has had time to explore these experiences separately, bring them together to share major insights from the other group's discussion. If differences come to light, explore these. Keep the conversation open-ended and accepting of different points of view. There are no "right" answers here; we do not know what really happened.

Women Followers of Jesus Discuss Their Actions

As a woman in Jesus' time, your testimony in any Jewish court would be discredited because of "the levity and rashness of (your) sex."

Answer the following questions:

1. Why did you start to follow Jesus in the first place?
2. Why did you follow him to Jerusalem?
3. Why did you go to watch the crucifixion of Jesus?
4. Why did some of you go with Joseph of Arimathea to see where Jesus was laid?
5. You have just found the tomb to be empty and heard the message from the young man at the tomb. What did you first think? How did you first feel? What did you first do? What next?
6. Who did you tell? How did they respond? Did they believe you? What did you do after that?
7. As time passed, what happened to you who were women followers of Jesus? Where did you go? Why?
8. What happened to the male disciples? Why?

Male Disciples of Jesus Discuss Their Actions

As a male follower of Jesus, you might well have been arrested for helping to cause unrest and discontent among the people with their current government.

Answer the following questions:

1. Why did you first follow Jesus?
2. Why did you follow him to Jerusalem?
3. Why did you desert Jesus when he was arrested in the garden of Gethsemane? What were you feeling? What were you thinking about?
4. Peter, when you were in the courtyard of Pilate, why did you deny that you knew Jesus? What were you afraid of?
5. Why did none of you go to Golgotha when Jesus was crucified? How did you feel about not going? Where did you go after Jesus was arrested? Why?
6. When the women came to tell you that Jesus had risen, what did you think? How did you respond to them?
7. When did you first believe that Jesus was somehow "still alive and going before you"? What caused you to believe?
8. As time passed, what happened to you? Why?
9. What happened to the women followers as time passed? Why?

(I) Continue to write in journals.

- Invite students to respond in their journals to the following questions:
—What do you believe about the empty tomb?
—What does it mean to us in the twentieth century that Jesus "is going before you into Galilee"?
- After time for personal writing, invite individuals to share from their writing if they wish—or to share general ideas and questions.

(J) A last look at Mark's understanding of Jesus and our understanding of Jesus.

- Read again Mark 1:15 where Mark states his major thesis about Jesus.
- Review the Dimension 3 material in the study book.
- As a large group answer the following questions:
—What is the "good news"?
—Is Mark trying to "prove" his thesis in the rest of his book? If not, what is Mark trying to do in the rest of his Gospel?

—What is the meaning of the empty tomb at the end of Mark?

—What do you think about the message "he is going before you to Galilee"?

(K) Finish writing your modern gospel.

- Add a last chapter to your modern gospel, focusing on the telling of non-Christians today about Jesus' empty tomb.
—How will you leave the story?
—With what message do you want to leave your readers?
- If you have been writing this gospel on newsprint, decide what you will do with your writings.

(L) Sing Scripture.

- Listen to recorded selections (about the Resurrection) from *The Messiah*, *Godspell*, or *Jesus Christ Superstar*. Or sing the Shaker tune, "Lord of the Dance" (No. 261, *The United Methodist Hymnal*).
- Discuss how this music portrays the Resurrection. Do you agree with its interpretation?
- As an alternate activity, offer paint or clay or both to students to work with in a creative, impressionistic way while they are listening to the music.

(M) Hold a mock TV interview (a summary activity).

- Give each student the name of one of the persons in the Gospel of Mark who met Jesus. (See the sidebar.)
- Ask students then to study one character's interaction with Jesus for the purpose of identifying key feelings and learnings about Jesus from that interaction.
- Interview each character, using the following questions:
—How did you know Jesus?
—What do you remember about Jesus?
—How did you feel about your interaction?
—What is the major insight or learning you gained from Jesus?
- After the mock TV interview, ask the class to reflect on what they have heard.

TEACHING TIP

If the class is large, assign two or more people to each biblical character to do their research. Ask one person to serve as spokesperson for the biblical character. To build on the "interview" quality of this activity, use a microphone or facsimile. You might "set the stage" like a late night talk show with chairs and a desk. If someone has a video camera, you might even tape the interviews.

Characters/Related Scriptures for TV Interview

John the Baptist (Mark 1:1-8; 6:14-29)
Simon Peter (Mark 1:16; 1:36-37; 3:16; 4:33-41; 5:37; 6:7 and 30; 6:35; 6:49; 7:17; 8:27-30; 9:2-13; 9:33-37; 13:3; 14:17, 26, 32, 37, 50, 54, 66-72)
James and John (Mark 1:19; 4:33-41; 5:37; 6:7; 6:35; 6:49; 7:17; 8:27; 9:2-13; 9:33-40; 10:35-40; 13:3; 14:17, 26, 32, 50)
the women followers (Mark 1:36; 2:18; 3:7; 3:34; 4:33-41; 6:1; 7:17; 8:27; 10:1; 10:17; 10:32; 15:40-41; 15:47; 16:1-8; 16:9)
the man with an unclean spirit (Mark 1:23-28)
Simon Peter's mother-in-law (Mark 1:30-31)
a leper (Mark 1:40-45)
the paralyzed man (Mark 2:3-12)
the friends of the paralyzed man (Mark 2:3-12)
a man with a withered hand (Mark 3:1-6)
Jesus' mother (Mark 3:31; 15:40-41; 15:47; 16:1-8)
Mary Magdalene (15:40-41; 15:47; 16:1-8)
an unclean spirit from the tombs (Mark 5:2-20)
Jairus (Mark 5:21-43)
Jairus' daughter (Mark 5:21-43)
the woman with the flow of blood (Mark 5:25-34)
the Gentile woman's daughter with an unclean spirit (Mark 7:24-30)
the deaf man in the Decapolis (Mark 7:31-37)
the blind man at Bethsaida (Mark 8:22-26)
the man with the epileptic child (Mark 9:14-29)
the rich young man (Mark 10:17-22)
Bartimaeus, the blind beggar (Mark 10:46-52)
the thoughtful scribe (Mark 12:28-34)

Closing Prayer

Magnificent, mysterious, ever-loving God we are amazed, we are afraid, we are cautious, we are threatened, we are thankful, we are full of praise and wonder, we are hopeful for yet another chance to understand your will and your ways. You are truly amazing in your patience with our unbelieving, contradictory ways. Continue to open our eyes and our ears as we come forth now to follow Jesus, who has promised that he is "going ahead of us into Galilee." In Jesus' name we pray, Amen.

Additional Bible Helps

Was There a Lost Ending of Mark?

Was Mark's ending the "real" ending? Did Mark leave the women terrified and fleeing from the empty tomb? If so, why? Was Mark employing a writer's technique to say to readers "of course we know that they must have told the disciples because here we are talking about it all!" Maybe. And maybe Mark wrote that ending as a way to say to his first listeners that the response is finally up to each person: what do you believe about this man Jesus? Will you follow him as he goes before you back into Galilee? It is a theory that makes a lot of sense.

But another theory also makes some sense. That is the theory that the first and "real" ending of Mark was lost. This theory does not necessarily discredit what we have of Mark. It just says: that is not the whole story!

Of course the women were afraid! Whether they went to anoint a dead body for burial or just to grieve beside the tomb, the empty tomb and the appearance or vision of a heavenly messenger saying "Jesus is not here—he has gone ahead of you to Galilee" would be enough to strike fear in anyone's heart.

But beyond this fear, the women had other reasons to be terrified. In the noncanonical Gospel of Peter (12:50—13:57) the writer notes:

Now early on the Lord's day, Mary Magdalene, a disciple of the Lord—*who was afraid because of the Jews, for they were inflamed with anger* and had not done at the tomb of the Lord the things which women usually do to their loved ones when they die—took friends with her, and came to the tomb where he was laid. *And they feared lest the Jews see them*, and said, "Even if we were not able to weep and lament him on the day on which he was crucified, yet let us now do so at his tomb. But who will roll away the stone for us that is set against the door of the tomb, that we may enter and sit beside him and perform our obligations?" For the stone was large. *We fear lest someone see us.* But if we cannot, then let us lay beside the door the things which we have brought in remembrance of him, and we will weep and lament until we get home." And they went and found the tomb open; and they went near and looked in there, and saw there a young man sitting in the middle of the tomb, handsome, and dressed in a brilliant robe. And he said to them, "Why have you come? Whom do you seek? Not him who was crucified, for he has risen and gone. But if you do not believe it, look in and see the place where he lay, that he is not here. For he has risen and gone to the place from which he was sent." *Then the women were afraid and fled.*

(From *Gospel Parallels*, by Burton Throckmorton; page 187. Italics added.)

The women were afraid, not just of a divine manifestation or at the lack of a body, but also of the Jewish authorities who had arrested Jesus and manipulated his death. If those authorities saw them around the tomb, what might they do to them?

British biblical scholar Morna Hooker in *The Gospel According to Saint Mark* says it is part of the "scandal of the gospel" that the message of the Resurrection was entrusted to a group of women, for "even if they had delivered it, their words would have had no value, since Jewish law demanded the evidence of two male witnesses to establish anything!" Hooker concludes: "It is ironic that on Easter morning those who had faithfully followed Jesus to his crucifixion should flee from the tomb—just as the disciples fled from arrest (14:50, 52): this stupendous act is too great even for their loyalty" (page 393).

Was the empty tomb "too great even for their loyalty"? Or was it too threatening to their very lives? In first century Jewish law-courts the testimony of women was discredited because of the "levity and rashness of their sex." No one would believe them. What would happen *to them* if they made this wild claim that Jesus was still alive? They too were part of this motley band of people whose leader had been contradicting the Jewish leaders, causing crowds to gather, and raising discontent with the established ways of doing things. Remember that the Jewish leaders wanted Jesus dead. Maybe they wanted his followers dead too? Or punished? Wouldn't you be afraid? At least in the first moments? So the ending of Mark that we have (16:1-8) can be read at least two different ways.

The theory of the lost ending proposes that there must have been more: Mark must have gone on to say what did happen with the women. One can speculate on what the "lost" part said—about the women's actions after their original moments of fear—and about how their amazing witness would have been received by the male disciples. Even more interesting is the question: Why would this "lost" ending get lost?

Basic Tools for Bible Study

By Jack Keller

The Bible is the church's book. Therefore we call the Bible *Scripture*. The Bible is the authoritative guidebook for the church. But many people in the church have trouble claiming the Bible as their own. "It's so hard to understand." "It's so complex that we're intimidated."

How can you get past those objections? How can you help your church recover your own foundational book? Part of the answer is to identify, to use, and to teach others how to use some basic tools for Bible study. These are tools that laypeople can learn to wield with skill.

The Bible

The first and most important tool is a Bible you can mark as you read. I think *The HarperCollins Study Bible* (HarperCollins, 1993) is the best study Bible now available that uses the New Revised Standard Version. It provides explanatory comments as well as cross-references and maps. Whichever version you choose to use as your primary Bible, have several translations close at hand. Sometimes the alternative translations of a term or verse give clues about where to dig in. But beware of paraphrases such as the *Living Bible*. Paraphrases put the reader at the mercy of the one who did the paraphrasing. If he or she has misinterpreted a text, then everyone reading it misses the message.

The most important step in any type of Bible study is to read the biblical text itself as *if you were seeing it for the first time*. As Robin Maas, founder of the Lay Resource Center at Wesley Theological Seminary, points out in her excellent *Church Bible Study Handbook* (Abingdon, 1982; out of print but still available in some church libraries), *"the single greatest obstacle to understanding scripture is the sincere conviction on the part of the reader that he or she already knows what the text means simply because it sounds so familiar"* (page 131).

That presumption short-circuits the power of the Bible to challenge and to provoke us.

Take as an example Jesus' parable of the good Samaritan (Luke 10:29-37). Who is the neighbor in this story? Most people would answer, "the man who was beaten and left half-dead." From that answer to the generalization that our neighbor is anyone in need is an easy step. That principle may be sound, but it misses some of the punch in this parable. Look at the text again. The neighbor is actually the Samaritan who rescued the beaten man. Think how that idea, a Jew accepting aid from a despised Samaritan, must have shocked Jewish ears. It would be bad enough to be left helpless but even worse to be utterly dependent on the compassion of one's enemy, or so the situation must have seemed to Jesus' listeners. The message about neighbor love is richer than most of us suppose. And we miss that deeper meaning unless we carefully discover what the biblical text really says.

All of the other reference tools you use are simply means by which you discover the meaning of the text. To suppose you know it all at the start is to deprive yourself of Scripture's treasure.

Theological Wordbooks

Many of the terms used in the Bible are deceptive. You think you know what they mean, but you may miss the richer connotations of the original Hebrew or Greek. So a theological workbook is an essential Bible study tool. One of the best is *A Theological Word Book of the Bible*, edited by Alan Richardson (Macmillan, 1962).

Take an example. Under the entry for "know, knowledge" you find that the Hebrew term translated as *know* means much more than intellectual knowledge. It means to *have experience* of something or someone. *To know God*, then, means much more than to know information or theories about God; it means that you intimately experience God in your life.

Bible Dictionaries

The world the Bible describes is in many respects an alien world. It is strange because it is unknown. As a careful reader you will not want to gloss over that alien character, to assume too quickly that you know what was going on in those ancient days. Bible dictionaries can help. More like small-scale encyclopedias than traditional dictionaries, Bible dictionaries have a wealth of information about the people, events, ideas, and books of the Bible.

Examine the Pharisees as one example. Many people have an image of the Pharisees as the bad guys. But a quick look in a Bible dictionary reveals that the Pharisees were in many respects the moral and religious examples of their society. Many among them were much like the Christian pillars of our churches today—thoroughly respectable, good, decent, and God-fearing people. The Gospel stories sound a little different once you realize that Jesus' warnings against the Pharisees in his day may fit your church members rather well!

Bible dictionaries vary in size and depth. The new standard for comprehensive coverage is *The Anchor Bible Dictionary* (Doubleday, 6 volumes, 1992). *The Interpreter's Dictionary of the Bible* (Abingdon, 4 volumes, 1962; supplementary volume, 1976) is older but still found in some church libraries. Two solid recent examples of affordable, single-volume dictionaries are *The Dictionary of Bible and Religion,* edited by William H. Gentz (Abingdon, 1986), and *Harper's Bible Dictionary,* edited by Paul J. Achtemeier, (Harper and Row, 1985).

Bible Handbooks

Bible handbooks help keep you from losing sight of the forest while in the trees. They typically present a thumbnail sketch of the content and context of each book of the Bible. Most versions also include essays on all sorts of background material on various subjects from ancient measures, weights, money, and calendars to ancient manuscripts to archeology. Two examples with somewhat different theological slants are *Eerdmans' Handbook to the Bible,* edited by David Alexander and Pat Alexander (Eerdmans, 1983) and *The Illustrated Bible Handbook,* by Edward P. Blair (Abingdon, 1987). The latter is out of print, but found in some church libraries. A helpful recent volume, which serves some of the same purposes as a handbook, is *A Beginner's Guide to the Books of the Bible,* by Diane L. Jacobson and Robert Kysar (Augsburg/Fortress, 1991).

Books That Introduce the Bible

General introductions weave more history into the explanations about the content and development of the Scriptures than is found in Bible handbooks. But the usefulness is similar: to get a sense of the big picture within which a particular passage is located. Bernhard W. Anderson's much-used *Understanding the Old Testament* is now in its fourth edition (Prentice-Hall, 1986). I also like Peter C. Craigie's *The Old Testament: Its Background, Growth, and Content* (Abingdon, 1986). Craigie takes special pains to explain fairly where and why conservative and liberal biblical scholars disagree. For the New Testament, James L. Price's *The New Testament: Its History and Theology* (Macmillan, 1987) is a standard reference work. Other good options are also in print.

Concordances

A concordance to the Bible is another basic tool for Bible study. Many people use a concordance only when they want to look up a half-remembered verse that keeps nagging their memory. But a concordance has a systematic place in Bible study too.

Suppose you want to study a theme such as *redemption* (perhaps because it cropped up in a passage you were reading). A concordance will tell you where to find *redemption* in the Bible.

Be sure to select a concordance that you can use with your translation of the Bible. Concordances are available for use with the following versions of the Bible: King James Version, New Revised Standard Version, Revised Standard Version, New International Version, and *Good News Bible: The Bible in Today's English Version.*

Bible Atlases

Another type of resource that can help is an atlas of Bible lands. Even a quick look at a map can help you place a biblical passage in a geographic location and therefore make better sense of it. You may, for example, be able to picture the setting of Psalm 137 when you see how far Babylon was from Jerusalem. A map of the Mediterranean world is necessary if you are trying to keep track of the travels and letters of Paul.

Many Bible-map resources are available. Probably the standard reference is the *Oxford Bible Atlas,* third edition, edited by Herbert G. May (Oxford University Press, 1985). The twenty-six detailed maps are accompanied by short essays explaining the linkages to biblical texts and general background. More ambitious readers may want to peruse *The Harper Atlas of the Bible,* edited by James B. Pritchard (Harper and Row, 1987), which is available in oversized and concise editions.

Commentaries

What about commentaries on the Bible? There is no question that commentaries can help you. But they can be dangerous, too, in a couple of ways. First, you can easily become dependent on commentaries and never do the homework necessary to know a text for yourself. Second, when you lean heavily on selected commentaries, you are at their mercy. If the scholar in your favorite commentary misses a point, you miss it too. If the scholar has a theological axe to grind, you may mistake a conclusion based on prejudice for a pure and simple exposition of the truth.

The insights of commentaries, however, are too valuable to give up entirely. But the proper time to consult them is *after* you have struggled with the text for a while and have reached a tentative interpretation. A commentary may confirm your insights. It may sound a warning against your going off the deep end with a false interpretation. Or a commentary may point out something crucial that you missed.

Beginning students of the Bible may want to consult a one-volume commentary on the whole Bible such as *Harper's Bible Commentary,* edited by James L. Mays (Harper and Row, 1988) or *The Interpreter's One-Volume Commentary on the Bible,* edited by Charles M. Laymon (Abingdon, 1971). The paperback *Basic Bible Commentary* (Abingdon, 29 volumes, 1994) also offers guidance to beginners in an affordable format.

To dig deeper, you will need to consult a multi-volume critical commentary. I strongly recommend the 12-volume *New Interpreter's Bible* (Abingdon, 1994-2000), which has been explicitly designed to make biblical scholarship accessible and useful to clergy and laity in the churches. But there are strong volumes in several other critical commentary series, as well. Whenever possible, it is best to consult more than one commentary. No single perspective can capture all of the meanings and significance in a particular biblical book or passage.

Because of the expense involved, most individuals can accumulate a personal library of commentaries only over a long period of time. One alternative is to pool the purchases of members of a class or study group, making them available for common use. Another alternative is to build a collection of commentaries to which everyone has access in your church's library.

When all is said and done about tools for Bible study, the Bible is still the most important resource. No matter how useful secondary sources can be, it would be a great mistake to let reference tools absorb more attention than the Bible itself. So use the tools to help unlock the riches of Scripture but keep clearly in mind which book is the real treasure chest.

Jack Keller is Reference Books Editor for Abingdon Press. Adapted from *Leader in the Church School Today,* Fall 1988; pages 20-22. Copyright © 1988 by Graded Press.

The World of the Bible: African Origins

"As an African American, I get tired of the endless efforts to recast the biblical record into an ancient religious drama of Euro-Asian Hebrews.

"I get weary with those who would turn the biblical record into a tale of distinctly non-African people who briefly sojourned in Egypt (which was somehow removed from Black Africa) before moving on to ancient Canaan, which, despite its location, also had no relation to Africa. . . .

"The surprise for many of us is that the Bible itself reflects a genuine multiculturalism. Its pages are laced with racial and ethnic diversity. . . .

"I put this forward as an invitation for all of us to rediscover the lost multicultural biblical world, a discovery which will do much to help us live more authentically and more biblically in our own rapidly emerging global village. . . .

"*Afrocentricity* [a term coined by professor Molefi Kete Asante, chair of the African American studies department at Temple University] is simply the idea that

Window in Mulungwishi Chapel, Zaire

Linda Tanquist Boulos

Africa—and persons of African descent—must be seen as proactive subjects within history rather than as passive objects of Western triumphalism. . . . [It] means reestablishing Africa and her descendants as centers of value, without in any way demeaning other people or their historic contributions to world civilization."

With these words Professor Cain Hope Felder lays out his premise of the African origins not only of Jesus but also of much of the biblical world. He notes, for example, that recent studies of ancient icons as well as new insights into the importance of Egyptian and Ethiopian cultures and civilizations point to darker-skinned images of Jesus' mother, Mary, as being more ancient and therefore probably more accurate. Says Felder, "Mary undoubtedly looked like any other Afro-Asiatic woman living in Nazareth." And so, therefore, did Jesus and many of the "native" peoples that Jesus meets in his ministry in Palestine.

Moses, says Felder, was most likely an Afro-Asiatic

leader married to an Ethiopian woman (Numbers 12:1-10). King Solomon (an ancestor of Jesus) married the daughter of an Egyptian pharaoh. Mary and Joseph fled with the child Jesus to Egypt where, Felder notes, "they apparently can blend into the crowd—and live in safety."

Furthermore, Felder reminds us that the area of the world that we call the ancient land of Canaan and which we know today as "the Middle East" was, "culturally and geographically, primarily an extension of the African land mass." The "fertile crescent" of the Tigris and Euphrates rivers served as a gateway to Asia for ancient African peoples. Certainly some European peoples were there (Romans and Greeks), but they appear often in roles of oppressors of the native Afro-Asian peoples.

Citing these and other observations and facts about African origins and various reasons for the "de-Africanizing" of the biblical world, Felder concludes: "by modern Western standards, the earliest biblical people would have to be classified as 'Blacks.' They had a definite measure of African blood—and clearly resembled many individuals who would today be identified as African Americans."

How did we get to the place where we view Jesus as Semitic (a term that was not even invented until the nineteenth century) or "Middle Eastern"? Artists contributed to one part of the process when, over centuries, they sought to please powerful European leaders by continually lightening the paint they used to portray biblical persons.

Why is it important that we all—Black and White—begin to recover the African origins of our biblical story? In this day of escalating ethnic rivalries and bloodshed around the world, we desperately need the liberating image of a genuine multiculturalism in our biblical story. We need the liberating voices of Asians, Native Americans, Hispanics, and African Americans (as well as Europeans and Americans) to raise the good news of God's inclusive love and forgiveness.

Adapted from the article, "Out of Africa I Have Called My Son," by Cain Hope Felder, in the Nov.-Dec. 1992 issue of The Other Side, *300 W. Apsley, Philadelphia, PA 19144. Used by permission.*

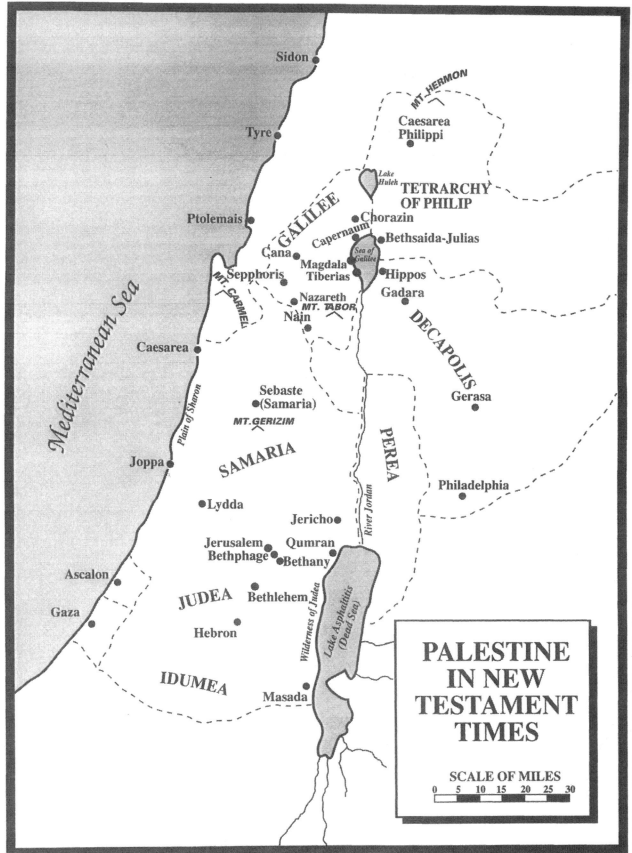

PALESTINE IN NEW TESTAMENT TIMES

SCALE OF MILES

0 5 10 15 20 25 30

47631288R00044

Made in the USA
Middletown, DE
29 August 2017